Circe's Cauldron

Pagan Poems and Tales of Magic and Witchcraft

Edited by Rebecca Buchanan

To the weavers of words and will
And the Powers who taught them,
and teach us still

L'Envoûteuse (The Sorceress)
by Georges Merle

Table of Contents

I confess: I am a fantasy geek. I read more fantasy novels and short stories (of every subgenre) than I do any other genre of literature. I love stories about Gods and Goddesses and witches and knights, epic quests, valiant stands against evil, and desperate bids to save the world — or maybe just save dinner from a brownie gone bad.

And there are a *lot* of fantasy stories out there. *A lot.* But very, very few of them address the genre from a pagan, polytheist point of view. For most authors, this is just an exercise in imagination. Fun, definitely, for both the author and the reader. But nothing more.

For those who actively believe in the Gods and Goddesses, for those who actively practice magic, however — ah, that is a different story.

For us, Brigid and Circe and Hekate and Odin and Taliesin are not characters. They are not fictional beings to be manipulated, tossed around, mocked, or satirized. They are very real. And the stories we tell about them — whether ancient or modern creations — are a form of worship; or, at the very least, a show of respect on our part and an acknowledgement of their power. These are contemporary myths, and they bring the Gods and Goddesses and witches and heroes into the world right alongside us.

The poems and tales in this collection cover a wide range of styles, but are fairly narrow in their focus. Perhaps not surprisingly, most deal with the pantheons of Europe; Circe and Hekate are particularly popular. Only a few address Deities from Egypt and Mesopotamia. And while most celebrate the Powers That Be, a few also offer cautionary examples, reminding us that we are dealing with beings who have their own agency, their own agenda, and that their interests do not always align with those of mortals.

It is my hope that *Circe's Cauldron* will be the first in a series, and that future volumes will continue to expand in their focus. I would be delighted to see modern myths which celebrate Hekate and Freyja alongside those which honor Kamrušepa, Oya, and Bluetongue Lizard.

For now, find a quiet moment to sit down and lose yourself in these poems and tales of Gods and Goddesses and witches and wizards — after all, stories are magic.

Rebecca Buchanan
Winter 2020

P.S. For those who are curious, there is an appendix which includes brief entries on the Deities and other figures referenced in this anthology.

The Alchemist's Side of the Story

by Marie C Lecrivain

I stood in the doorway, and I saw her.
The lovely Circe with the braided hair.
          — The Odyssey (*)

I.
You intrude upon my solitude.
And yes, I know no woman
is an island. Misogyny stings
like nettles embedded
in my hands. So I smile,
toss my braids in *that* way
and tell you, "Why, yes, my darlings,
I can't survive without you."

II.
You and your brothers invade
like a flood burst. Heavy, brutish,
and reeking of boredom,
you root through my home
like pigs searching for truffles
among the leaves and destroy
the peace I've worked so hard
to weave. You help yourself
to the fruits of my hard-won
labors, imbibing this and that;
it's what you'd do at home.

It's the order of *your* world.

III.
You demand more … and still more.
I descend into the darkest part
of my larder to fetch the best
of what remains; a bittersweet
draught brewed during the dark
of the moon, and slowly distilled
through seven years of silence.
Added to the last flagon of wine,
I watch as each drop is devoured
with greedy gulps until you
collectively collapse in
a drunken heap on the floor.

IV.
I'd like to watch what happens
as noses flatten,
fingers and toes fuse,
spines shorten and
shoulders recede,
but this part of the process
is best left alone. When I hear
the first panicked squeals,
my work is done.

*Excerpted from **The Odyssey**, Book 10: The Winds and The
Witch, Homer, translated by Emily Wilson, © 2018

Allegory

by James B. Nicola

Why, come into the shade and rest awhile,
My dear, said the crone with the winning
       smile,
The sun has been burning on your face,
She purred with an other-worldly grace
In dulcimer tones, But here, my sweet,
You can escape from the light and heat.
So bright and so hot was the day that he,
Eyes dripping with sweat, could barely see
The thing that drew him under a tree
And into the cave of shade. They went
Deep in the dark, then she left the gent,
Stranding him there where he has spent
The oblivious life of a pampered prince,
Insignificant, ever since.

*[Previously published in **Pennsylvania Review**]*

<u>Aradia</u>

by Hayley Arrington

Born of moonlight
torch flame
and shooting stars

Born of loam
moss
and ancient groves

Born of libations
seafoam
and sweat upon the brow

Primordial Priestess
Diana's Daughter
Goddess of Magic
Mystery
Mirth

Aradia
I whisper your name
My magic is great because of you
May my magic rites find favor in your eyes

Brigid

by Lee Clark Zumpe

home in your apple orchard
        on the far side of the Otherworld
        your sweet perfume in the air
calling bees to collect magical nectar;

I see you in the Fire of the Hearth,
        patroness of healing and fertility
        attendant of Spring
after the long reign of the Cailleach;

I see you in the Fire of the Forge,
        patroness of smithcraft,
        mother to craftsmen
and forger of Excalibur;

I see you in the Fire of Inspiration,
        patroness of poetry,
        subtle muse and custodian of verse
channeling wisdom through willing scribes.

<u>Ceridwen</u>

by Rebecca Buchanan

Crooked woman, they call me.
Arrogant poets! They do
not understand, and think it
a slight on my character.

I am *crooked*, yes, because
I bend, twist, shift my shape, and
— sometimes — change others into
forms more beautiful, more true.

But not him, my beloved
son. His hideous shape I
could not change. I could never
make him fair, no, not like the

little boy who called him friend
and ran with him through the woods
and flowering fields. But my
beloved son's mind — his mind! —

that I could re-form, re-mold,
re-fashion into something
bright and splendid. So I took
up my great silver cauldron

and set it upon flames of yew
and hawthorn and ash. I filled
it with the clear waters of
Mother Dôn's own river, the

quickness of a hare and the
keenness of a greyhound, the
radiance of a salmon
and the sleek nimbleness of

an otter, the song of a
lark and the tenacity
of a hawk. Last, I placed one
green kernel of unripened

wheat atop the seething brew.
I set the fair little boy
beside the flames, a spoon of
rowan in his hands, and showed

him how to stir the brew. Sun
followed sun, moon followed moon.
I dared not sleep. For a year,
every dawn and every dusk,

I set aside my work to
study the tiny grain, while
the boy continued to stir
and stir and stir the potion.

But then exhaustion claimed me.
I wrapped my glossy feathered
cloak around my shoulders and
lay down beside the flames. In

my weariness, I slept through
the dawn and did not see the
grain turn bright and gold. The boy
— oh, foul child! — did not

awaken me. The seed cracked
open, shedding three drops of
the sacred brew. They splashed the
boy's thumb. He dropped my rowan

spoon and then — oh, foul thief! —
licked the potion from his burnt
finger. I awoke then, too
late, and saw what he had done.

His mind opened, he fled. He
ran from me, desperate to
escape my wrath. Crooked, he
bent his shape, becoming a

hare. I took the form of a
greyhound, my dark eyes keen. He
twisted his shape, becoming
a salmon. I took the form

of an otter, my fingers
nimble. He shifted his shape,
becoming a lark. I took
the form of a hawk, swift and

tenacious in my pursuit.
He fell from the sky into
a gleaming field of wheat, one
grain among multitudes. I,

the crooked woman, bent and
twisted and shifted my shape
and became a black hen, my
feathers glossy, my beak sharp.

He could not escape me. I
swallowed him whole. My potion
lost, my scheme for naught, I doused
the flames with the clear waters

of Mother Dôn, scattered the
cold cinders of the yew and
hawthorn and ash, and tucked my
silver cauldron away. But

his trickery was not yet
ended and within a moon,
I knew that he had crooked his
shape once again. I vowed that,

as I had given him life,
so I would give him death. But
when he pushed himself loose from
my womb, singing, his eyes bright,

his face shining, I could not
bring myself to extinguish
the wonder that I had brought
into the world. But neither

could I feed him at my breasts,
hold him in my arms, kiss him,
as I did my beloved
son — the brother he had so

cruelly robbed. So I gathered
birch and willow and ivy
and built a coracle. I
filled it with soft ferns and sweet

apple leaves. I laid him in
his bed and cast him upon
the clear waters of Mother
Dôn. I turned my back. I did

not watch as the wide river
carried him away, but I
heard him singing, singing his
new true name: Taliesin.

Circe, Starweaving

by Clarabelle Fields

hot, with sweat damp on her forehead
she takes a pause and sits
beside her harvest,
a basket of newborn stars,
some silvery-fresh, still budding
others already beginning to bloom
with a silent, trembling warmth

she turns them over with tired hands
her face and her cheeks and her clothes
alive with scintillating stardust
and dusky night-soil, the indigo ink
of sky-fabric lining the insides of her nails,
sketching patterns in her palms and wrists,
melting into veins, paths that wind
up her arms and around her heart
and into the hungry hollow below her throat
where her pulse runs thick and quick,
quickening as stars brush together
and murmur in icy, satin voices,
a whisper that picks up cold along her skin
and the sky parts, a million diamonds
cupped in two ancient hands

she is suddenly small, one among many,
craning her neck to take in
the boundless sweep of obsidian
the dark beyond the dark:
and at its core, one large, weeping, glaring
eye and the heavy brow of She
Who Plaited These Stars
stringing them on her own silver hair
beside their mothers and grandmothers
and all stars born before and after

She was the one who knelt over
the primordial stirring pot,
breathing life into the bellies of stars
and eventually men and even
the little starstricken witch in her shadow,
a basket by her bare feet

"Go home," the Mother says, her voice a wave
of wind, ocean, and time
and Circe runs through the dark,
the warmth of another's breath on her back,
leaving a trail of broken stars
tumbling behind her

Daoine Sidhe

by Lee Clark Zumpe

Finbheara,
King under the fairy hill of Knockma:
What has become of you?

In Connaught
We once held some sway;
Now they claim our kind has gone away.

With mischief banned
We can't play tricks on little girls
Or kick up clouds of dusty swirls;

Or disturb dreamers
In the twilight hour,
Or even make the milk go sour!

Bound by laws
Which I abhor,
We can't steal children anymore!

No more frolicking,
It seems our merriment is through;
Oh, what's a fairy king to do?

Fleurs du Mal

by Ed Ahern

Jamie swallowed the dregs from the bottle of wine he'd opened an hour earlier, then spoke.

"I wish you still drank. You were less serious."

Paul snorted. "Don't keep flogging the same ex drunk. You know I had to stop. I'm headed home. If you remember, tell Claudia I said good night."

"I sometimes think you still come over here so you can look at Claudia."

"I sometimes think you're right."

Jamie heaved out of his chair. "Agh, Paul, god damn it, stay, you're the only person I can open up to."

"We'll talk when you're sober. I'm home tomorrow if you want to stop by."

Paul's bachelor-sized cape cod was two blocks from Jamie's house. The atomized effect of Jamie's wine lingered on his skin. *I wonder*, he thought, *if I took a sip by osmosis?*

The next morning, Paul was halfway through his second cup of coffee when the mail flap on the front door chattered. He scooped up the printed flotsam, walked over to the waste basket, and began throwing pieces away.

One envelope caught his attention, written in heavy script and sealed with grape-purple wax. He broke the seal and pulled out a card twice the thickness of the envelope.

Mr. Paul Freeman and one guest are invited to sample the most recent bottling of Fleurs Du Mal. The tasting will be on the twelfth day of June, at seven o'clock in the evening. Arrangements have been made to take Mr. Freeman and guest at six o'clock in the evening from his domicile to the vignoble.

Hermes Treblewise

The invitation was absurd. He'd never heard of Fleurs Du Mal, and anyone who knew him knew that he didn't drink anymore. But the paper quality was better than any wedding invitation Paul had ever received. He carried it and a coffee refill with him into his back yard garden.

An hour later, Jamie's apologies preceded him into the yard. "Jesus, Paul, I'm sorry. I'm getting to be a weekend wino. Whatever I said, I didn't mean it …."

Paul sighed. "I can't figure out why Claudia stays with you. It's sure as hell not your drunken charm. You need to quit before it gets serious."

Jamie tensed, then relaxed. "We can't all be abstainers like you." He dropped into a lawn chair next to Paul and noticed the invitation. "Wow. Nice paper. Hand laid linen, I think. See the wire marks? And the ink. Looks almost medieval. Did you know they used to make ink from dried hawthorn branches or pounded gallnut? This has got that same gray-brown tint to it."

"And how the hell do you know this?

"I'm not your editor for nothing. Just for pitifully little. But I do know about paper and ink. Fleurs du Mal? I've heard hints about it. It's a liquor. Never sold commercially, doled out a bottle at a time to the select few. You've got to go!"

"I've got to not go. I'm a drunk, remember? You of all people don't want me acting like I used to."

"Yeah, but still, it says 'and friend.' You could take me, and I'll make sure you don't drink."

"It's got to be a mistake. I'd call and tell them, but there's no phone number or address."

Jamie slowly waved the invitation. "Aren't you curious? About how you got picked? About Hermes and his booze? You don't have to drink, I'll tell you about it."

"Just what I'm afraid of."

"Look, if you get goosey, start feeling trapped, I'll pay for a taxi home. We can't pass up this chance."

"We? Watch me."

He walked Jamie back over to his house and said hello to Claudia. Paul wanted to touch her, but didn't. Her leggy angularity was filling out nicely as she approached forty.

Claudia showed up at his house an hour later. "Jamie's mad that you're not taking him to a wine tasting."

"Hi, Claudia. That's poignantly tough shit, but your softening me up isn't going to change my mind. I'd go with you — you'd stay sober enough to make sure I didn't drink."

Claudia threw a well-remembered gaze at him.

"It's a big deal to him, Paul. You said your sobriety is pretty solid." She crossed her legs.

Paul's lips pursed. She'd always known how to barrage his senses. "It's a bad idea, Claudia. You shouldn't beg for him."

"It's not like that, Paul. It's just that what's important to him is important for me, too."

Paul shrugged. "All right. All right. For old time's sake. I should be able to survive for three hours. Tell Jamie we'll go."

Paul dithered about whether he should dress up or down. *If I dress up it seems important.* Casual it is. His AA sponsor had been adamant about his not going. But for the first time Paul had balked against his instructions. It seemed important to prove his sobriety.

Jamie and Paul's ride that Saturday evening was a black town car with darkened windows. The burly driver said he knew nothing other than the address, and that the trip would take a little less than an hour.

They stepped out of the car to face two stories of roughly dressed, quarter-ton stones topped with a slate roof. The narrow, deep-set windows were confined by black iron bars. Planted fields and hot houses surrounded the building. Paul recognized mountain laurel and lilies, daffodils and philodendron, Scotch broom and hemlock, but several hundred more species grew and flowered under glass panes or out in the open fields.

The driver told them he would bring them back in two hours. They crunched their way along a gravel walkway to a deeply inset door of thick wood slabs. Paul thought he saw oleander in one of the hot houses, and milkweed and bloodroot growing along the verge.

Jamie bounced with excitement. "This place looks like a little castle."

"Or a dungeon. It must be clammy as hell in there."

The door opened to their first knock. "Mr. Freeman. How I've anticipated your coming. And this is?"

"Jamie Carrington, my neighbor."

Hermes Treblewise's gauntness was masked under a black robe. The stubble on the top of his head advised that his monk's pate was self inflicted rather than genetic. His eyes were the color of mouse fur, indistinctly gray/brown. His handshake was aridly hot.

"Mr. Treblewise, I have to tell you from the onset that I no longer drink alcohol."

"Brother Treblewise, please. I knew that when I sent you the invitation, Mr. Freeman. But your prior reputation as a wine taster precedes you. I think you'll find my Fleurs Du Mal interesting."

"Not any more."

"Wait until you hear about it."

They sat in armchairs facing a stone fireplace. Inscribed stone slabs covered the floor, and the inside walls were the same rough-dressed stones as the outside. Despite the fire, the room was dank.

An ornate crest filled the wall above the fireplace mantel. Jamie tried to read the Latin lettering. "Tramagist, no that's not right. Trismagistus I think."

"Very good, Mr. Carrington. It's an obsolete spelling of my last name. Mr. Goodman, you're a gardener and amateur horticulturalist, so you'll appreciate my explanation. Some while ago I joined the Benedictine order and became one of their herbologists and vignerons —"

Jamie interjected. "Are you still Benedictine? I didn't notice any crosses in your house."

"Ah, no, regrettably my studies diverged from their requirements and I established my own little order. But no matter." Hermes crossed his legs. His feet were shod in open-toed sandals. His toe nails were completely black and snipped straight across.

"I wished to produce a liquor from flowers and berries. But not just some sickly-sweet grape brandy. I wanted to produce an elixir, a tonic that would make one drunk if enough was consumed, but that in moderation would give a man heightened, god-like sensitivities.

"There was no point in distilling from the usual suspects — pears or cherries or cloudberries. They'd all been used and only succeeded in getting one tipsy and sugar-overdosed.

"No, I went further afield, finding flowers and berries that had been ignored or detested. My initial efforts had unfortunate consequences, but I persevered. Now I need to provide my liquor to kindred spirits, to men teetering on the edge of a transformative experience. To you, Mr. Freeman." Treblewise paused. "I'm being ill mannered. Would you care for a glass of wine? The grapes are cultivated here at the vignoble."

Jamie answered without pause. "Yes, please. Is this the Fleurs Du Mal?"

"Ah, no, just our vin du table. And you Mr. Freeman?"

"I won't insult you by asking for a soft drink.   Just water please." Paul was interested despite himself, though, and asked, "So the plants and shrubs that we saw on the way in are used for the Fleurs Du Mal?"

"Yes. Each vintage is prepared to achieve a somewhat different effect, and the exact ingredients vary from year to year, to suit the intended drinkers."

Jamie finished off his glass of wine before Paul was halfway through his water. Treblewise poured Jamie another glass without asking.

"So, Mr. Freeman. Your prior achievements as an oenophile are the reason you received the invitation. A few small sips of Fleurs Du Mal will enhance your senses and awareness far beyond your most lucid moments. Great things have been done while under its influence. I would very much like for you to vary slightly from your non-use of alcohol and provide me with a report based on your educated palate."

The flattery was sinuous. Paul had written books about wines and cordials. Curiosity tugged at his taste buds. "No, Brother Treblewise, I'm sorry, but I can't do that. I am curious though: how did you decide to call this liquor Fleurs Du Mal?"

Treblewise visibly swallowed his displeasure at the refusal, then regained his manners. "Ah, yes, it's taken from a collection of poems by Charles Baudelaire. Do you read him? No? One of the poems in his book *Fleurs Du Mal* is about a monk. The last two stanzas in English would go something like:

My soul's a tomb, which-wretched friar! - I
Have paced since time began, and occupy:
Bare walled and hateful still my cloister
stands.

O slothful monk! When shall I learn to make
In the stark drama of a living mind
My special joy and work to fit my hands

"Baudelaire's poetry suits my temperament."

Jamie had been silent witness to the byplay. "But Paul, surely, in such small quantities you could provide a taste evaluation?"

Paul glowered. "No way in hell."

Treblewise studied them both and shrugged. "Well, Mr. Carrington, I believe that you are also familiar with wines and spirits, although perhaps not with quite the discerning palate of Mr. Goodman. How would it be if I were to give you a bottle of Fleurs Du Mal for your tasting? You should sip only very small quantities over many days, as otherwise the effects are deleterious."

"Absolutely!"

Treblewise turned to Paul. "I ask only that you observe the liquor's effect on Mr. Carrington and report back to me."

Jamie also turned his head toward Paul. "Please, Paul. You won't be tasting, just watching me drink — like you always do."

"Well, hell, all right, as long as I don't have to drink. How often do I have to report?"

"Once a week should do. I have no phone or internet, so you'll have to report in person. The driver will pick you up each week."

Treblewise left and returned with a green bottle. There was no label. He carefully opened the bottle with a bone-handled corkscrew, poured out a half ounce of the liquor, and held it out.

"Mr. Carrington, would you please affirm that you are accepting this libation of your own free will, without inducement or threat?"

"Yes, yes, of course."

As Jamie held the snifter before drinking, Treblewise continued. "The changes in your aptitudes and moods will be profound, Mr. Carrington. You'll literally become a different man. The effect will be both liberating and intoxicating. I'm required to remind you that overindulgence is quite dangerous. That's why you, Mr. Freeman, will be the one reporting back to me."

Already regretting his agreement, Paul said, "Don't do it, Jamie. Just put it down and we'll go home."

Jamie stared down at the minute amount of liquor in the snifter. "I could survive drinking this much paint thinner." He put his nose over the crystal and sniffed. "Wow. Really complex, Paul. I don't sense the alcohol, just flowers and berries."

He took a tiny sip and rolled it around his tongue and back onto his palette. He breathed several times through his nose. "It's like nothing else I've ever drunk. It's — I have no comparison, Paul. It's like drinking flower petals from an exotic garden. My tongue has opened up. I think I can taste my own saliva."

Treblewise's mouth squirmed into a smile meant only for himself. "Don't drink any more for some days, Mr. Carrington. And now, my good souls, your driver has arrived. Mr. Freeman, he'll pick you up at the same time next week? Detailed notes and descriptions, please."

The return trip was spent largely in silence. Jamie cradled the bottle, self-absorbed in new sensations. Paul wallowed in drunkard's remorse without knowing why he should feel guilty. "Jamie, don't drink any more of that stuff. I'll give him back the bottle next week."

"No way. I think my hormones just kicked into an overdrive. I haven't felt like this since high school. And my vision seems sharper."

"At least let me do some homework on this before you suck down another shot."

"Yeah, okay, sure." But Jamie was already distracted, focused inward.

Paul marched directly from his front door to the computer. Two hours later he called Jamie, but got Claudia.

"Claudia, how's Jamie?"

"Fine, I guess. He's just had another snifter from the green bottle and seems hyper-elated. Not drunk, but really wired."

"Jesus, put him on please."

A moment later: "Paul, it's incredible. I can almost taste colors. And I've thought my way out of a couple crappy problems at work. This stuff is the elixir of life."

"Like hell it is. Listen to me. Fleurs Du Mal doesn't mean *bad flowers*. It means *flowers of evil*. Every one of those plants we saw on the way in and out has poisonous flowers and berries. Every one. You're drinking plant poison. Dump it out."

"Like hell I will. Except for a few minutes of my honeymoon, I've never felt this good. And it's continuous. The second slug only made it better, stronger."

"*Second?* Listen to me. For God's sake, throw that shit away. Just save me a little so I can get it analyzed."

"Too late for you, buddy. No sips for you, just for me."

"Put Claudia back on …. Claudia? Don't let him touch that stuff again. I don't know what the hell we've gotten into, but I think that crap could kill him."

"He *is* different, Paul. More demanding. More self-absorbed. But he's not drunk and he doesn't look poisoned."

Phone still in hand, Paul started to go out the door and return to Treblewise's stone fortress, but realized that he had no idea of the routing they'd taken, just vague images filtered through the darkened glass of the limo.

After an hour's dithering, he walked over to Jamie's house. Claudia answered the door. She had hand-sized welts on her arms.

"He's not here. He took a third sip and left. I tried to stop him, but …." She waved her bruised arms. "I couldn't stop him. I don't know where he went." She started crying, soundlessly and without affectation.

Paul cupped her elbows and steered her back inside, then sat next to her on the sofa. He held her in silence for several minutes. "Where's the bottle, Claudia?"

"Jamie took it with him. He's like he used to get after snorting coke. His mind is racing so fast I don't think he can apply the brakes. He — he said things to me, Paul. And did things. Creepy, hurtful things. And I think he meant them."

"He loves you, Claudia, we know that. This damn liquor has short-circuited him. Did he take his cell phone?"

"Yes, but he told me not to call."

"I'll try to call him later."

Paul held her again, and this time Claudia put her arms around him. When the fading dusk had completely died, he shifted to face her and kissed her gently on the lips. It was as good as he remembered. "Once I find him, I'll break the bottle. I'm stronger than he is. Call me as soon as he gets back and I'll come over."

He called Jamie's phone after reaching home, but was dumped into voice mail. "Jamie, for Christ's sake, pick up. You've scared the shit out of Claudia and got me really worried. Call me as soon as you get this, no matter what time it is."

Paul fired up the computer and went into search mode on Hermes Treblewise, but got nowhere. Then he remembered Jamie's reading of the emblem in Treblewise's living room. Trismas? No, no Trismagistus. Lots on that son of a bitch. A legendary alchemist, drummed out of the Catholic Church several hundred years ago. He'd tried to develop an elixir of life from death-dealing plants, once poisoning off thirty of his followers with the assurance that they would be able to see God. And so they did, once they'd died.

And this crazy pseudo-monk is just as medieval as his namesake.

Paul called Jamie again a little after one in the morning and left another message, then went to bed. His cell phone went off two hours later.

"My eyes have seen such glories, Paul."

"Where are you, Jamie?"

"I'm riding a celestial dragon. Fleurs Du Mal! It's a tree of knowledge."

"Jamie, I can pick you up. Where are you?"

"I'm not going back to what I was. Oh, and Paul. You and Claudia. Take care of her. I told her you would."

"You're drunk."

"No, my friend, I'm lucent. The clarity is so piercing it hurts my bones."

The phone went dead. Paul redialed without success.

The next morning he drove over and picked up Claudia. They spent the day walking through neighborhoods that Jamie had once frequented to score drugs. Paul found himself twisting between fear for Jamie and perverse enjoyment of the time spent with Claudia. When he dropped her off, she started crying again. Paul hugged her tightly, vainly trying to squeeze in relief from her pain.

The next three days spiraled, following an identical pattern. They called Jamie's friends and fellow editors, visited police stations and hospitals in the morning, and in the afternoon and evening prowled unlikely places where he might have secreted himself.

The reassurance of words failed them, and they increasingly just touched and held each other. Paul kissed her morning and evening, his best pledge that she wasn't at fault and was still loved.

The hospital called the day before Treblewise's limo was scheduled to arrive. Jamie had washed ashore. They were at the intensive care ward within twenty minutes.

The doctor frowned at them as she explained the situation. "Mrs. Carrington, your husband is dangerously ill. We're flushing out his system, but our toxicology results are still coming back with dangerously high levels of various poisons. In his lucid moments, he's told us that this was self-administered through some kind of drink. Is this true?"

"Yes, doctor. Did they find a bottle with him?"

"According to police, he put up quite a fight when they took it away from him. Which is odd, because it was empty. We have him under suicide watch."

"Sweet Jesus," Paul blurted out, "he drank it all. But you're purging him?"

"Like I said. Um, Mrs. Carrington, he asked that you not be admitted to his room, but that he be awakened as soon as Mr. Freeman arrived. Are there domestic issues we should be aware of?"

Claudia's face, swollen from crying, congealed into lumpiness. She sobbed.

"Doctor, tell Jamie that I'll see him with Claudia or not at all."

Minutes later, they were in his room, the doctor and an orderly only a step behind. The poisons had sprouted open sores on Jamie's face and arms, and presumably over the rest of his body, as well. His eyes were the yellow of liver failure. He looked gaunt, but his mood was aggressive.

"Paul, when you see Treblewise tomorrow, tell him that I need two bottles this time."

Claudia started to cry again, but Jamie ignored her, staring intently at Paul.

"I'm not going back to Treblewise's, and I'm sure as hell not getting you any more of that liquor."

Jamie's shaking worsened. "It's an all-knowing, cosmic firework, Paul. I'm willing to flame out quickly. Just don't make me die in withdrawal."

"You're not going to die, but I hope you suffer like hell."

Jamie half flopped out of the bed, clutching at Paul. The orderly grabbed him and held him down on the bed.

"Restraints, doctor?"

"Yes, they're definitely indicated."

Claudia and Paul ate in the hospital cafeteria and drove back to her house. No conversation. No music. Paul found a bottle of wine, opened it, and brought her a glass. "It's not very good."

"I don't care. Paul, you have to go see that monk tomorrow."

"Not a chance."

"No, listen. If anyone knows what the antidote might be, he would. You have to ask him."

Paul poured her a second glass. They talked of minute, safe things. He leaned forward and kissed her again, not good night. Old memories took hold, and then resurged into familiar rhythms. Paul spent the night.

Over breakfast the next morning, they talked as if long married — of tending to Jamie, of Paul's trip to see the monk, their intimacy stored away in a curio cabinet.

The stoic limousine driver was punctual. Paul tried to question him about the address of the vignoble, about its direction, but the driver held silent. Once inside the limo, Paul noticed that the screen dividing him and the driver and the side and rear windows were almost completely opaque. As they started off, he pulled out his cell phone. It gave him an immediate error message, not even recognizing his current location.

Next time I have somebody follow us. Except there's no way there'll be a next time.

Treblewise again answered at the first knock. Paul exploded before he even stepped into the building. "Jamie's poisoned, maybe dying. You gave a drunk an alcoholic poison. I'm going to have you arrested."

"Ah, Mr. Freeman. Please do come in so we can talk in comfort."

Paul continued to storm as he walked inside. "You made this crap. What can he take to counteract its effects?"

"Nothing. However, the effects of a bottle of Fleurs du Mal drunk over several days might not kill him. A second bottle, drunk quickly, would assuredly be painfully fatal. I have two more bottles here.”

“That he’ll never get.”

Treblewise’s eyes developed a mustard tinge. “Don’t be obtuse, Mr. Freeman. Mr. Carrington is nothing special to me, just another tippler. You, however, roused my attention. You were a discerning taster and critic before you dried out and detoured.

“I’ll offer you a choice, Mr. Freeman. I’ll ensure that Mr. Carrington is never able to again drink Fleurs du Mal if you agree to sample it. I’ll pour you a drollop here and you take a bottle back with you. Mr. Carrington will probably recover, although I expect he’ll be scarred and bitter. As for yourself, you would just have to control the liquor and its visions.”

“Go to hell. I’ll never drink again. And I’ll make sure that Jamie doesn’t either.”

“You know better. My driver is extraordinarily devoted. He’ll have no trouble getting a bottle into Mr. Carrington’s willing hands. Think, Mr. Freeman. Is your *possible* loss of sobriety worth his *assured* death?”

“I’m not going to be blackmailed.”

“Very well, Mr. Freeman, since that’s your final answer.” Treblewise grinned. “Welcome back. Mr. and Mrs. Carrington can be told whatever you wish.”

“Welcome back?”

"Envy, pride, lust — more than adequate, and in only a few days. John 15:13, Mr. Freeman. Au revoir. We'll meet again."

The driver had silently entered the room. Paul wanted to wrestle Treblewise to the ground, but the driver would have beaten him down before he could accomplish anything. Treblewise smiled paternally as Paul raged out of the building.

He asked the driver to drop him at Claudia and Jamie's house. He shook with alternating surges of anger and fear.

Claudia was waiting for him. "Did you get the antidote?"

"No. We're going to have to guard Jamie. Treblewise has threatened to give him the liquor."

"Can we go to the police?"

"They wouldn't believe us, and there's nothing we could tell them that would help them find Treblewise. We have to get through this together." Paul put his arm gently around Claudia's waist and guided her back into the house.

Shortly after midnight he got up, went to Claudia's computer, and plugged in John 15:13. He could hear Treblewise mouthing the words.

Greater love has no one than this, that he lay down his life for his friends.

Paul stared without focus. *How the hell do I keep a raving addict away from his dealer? It's me*

Treblewise wants, not Jaime. If I agree to taste the Fleurs du Mal, would Treblewise have an antidote that would spare Jaime?

Claudia appeared in the doorway. "Are you coming back to bed?"

"In a minute. I'm thinking about having a drink."

Full Moon Over the Crossroads

by Gerri Leen

Hecate rides out of the west, the full moon just peaking over the mountains in the eastern distance. The wind blows cold and her hair streams behind her as she accelerates and heads the bike for the crossroads. She leans into the turns, enjoying the freedom of movement this current age offers.

Once upon a time she met her sisters on horseback, or by carriage or chariot, but this is so much more fun. The speed, the power underneath her — it's exhilarating. She knows Artemis feels the same. Selene? Who can say?

The sisters have always met on the night when the moon is full. Hecate's not the strongest of them tonight. Neither is Artemis. And as they ride out of the west and east, Hecate knows Artemis can feel Selene pulling on her the same way Hecate does. This is Selene's time.

The time of the fulsome moon, not just the full one. Days before and days after belong to her, too, and she milks them ruthlessly.

Soon Hecate will rule again. The dark of the moon, the waning light, will go with the black of her bike and the shadowy dark leathers she wears. Dust covers her boots from the crossroads she calls home and which they all agreed to meet at.

They meet here because Selene enjoys a biker bar situated not too far from the crossroads. She enjoys the bar — and its patrons — far too much for either Hecate's or Artemis's taste.

They will, in fact, have to pull Selene bodily from the bar if they want to ride as one tonight. And they always ride as one. It's how things are done. And Hecate is the old one — "how we've always done it" has merit with her.

Artemis likes to try new things but that does not extend to new lovers. Selene's appetites disturb her, so even though she might wish for the freedom to hunt with her hounds and nymphs tonight, she'll bow to the tried-and-true in order to get their sister away from some man draped in leather and drunk on Selene's appeal.

Hecate sees the crossroads ahead and slows. She's first to arrive. She's always first to arrive. She gets off the bike and walks off the asphalt, over to the dirt and sagebrush. "Come to me, my beauties," she murmurs, and soon she sees scorpions and tarantulas working their way to her. Even a sidewinder rouses herself to slither out to where Hecate waits. She crouches down and lets them walk and slide over her hands, listening to their tales of danger and hunting and how cold it is when the sun goes down.

From the east, she hears a bike approaching and tells her creatures to scatter, then stands up. Artemis is coming, and behind her, in the grass along the road race deer and coyotes. An owl slips overhead, winging silently at the sidewinder until Hecate holds up her hand and says, "You shall not."

The owl veers off; the snake is safe.

Artemis slides a bit on her stop, never losing control of the lithe sport bike, showing off as ever. Her skirt is short, her boots tall, and she has a bow and a quiver of arrows over her shoulder. She wears leather of light gray and dun, and her hair is as raven as Hecate's would be if it weren't shot through with gray. "Sister," she says, and Hecate sees a shiver of distaste in Artemis's expression as she looks at her.

She is everything that Hecate was, and Hecate is everything she will be. She waxes as Hecate wanes. They're the beginning and end — the Alpha and the Omega, as a prophet of the more popular god of the times has said. But Greek was their language before it was his. And Hecate speaks tongues even older than that.

"Where is she?" Artemis's expression is the one that mortals dread.

"Where do you think?" Hecate looks to the south.

"The roadhouse?"

Hecate nods.

"Why can't she just meet us? We agree every moon, at the end of the ride, to meet here."

"And she forgets as soon as the next moon comes, when her power grows and she can come out and play."

Artemis scowls. Her virginity is a badge of honor that she'll kill to hold onto. She views the idea of loving with distaste. Hecate remembers loving, but her body doesn't long for it any longer. Her need to nurture, to melt into another's arms, is long gone.

"We have to go get her." Artemis rolls her eyes.

"We do." Walking to her bike, Hecate mounts, pats down the crow feathers that form her headdress, and sees Artemis study them. "Not everything that's mine belongs to the night. Most of my creatures don't, in fact. That honor belongs to you and Selene." Hunting and mating are so often done under the moon's watchful gaze, not the blistering sun.

Artemis adjusts the deerskin headband she wears and revs her bike. She takes off to the south, not waiting for Hecate, but Hecate catches her little sister, easily keeping up with her so-fast-it's-probably-not-street-legal sport bike. Hecate's black and rust and chrome bike is much faster than it looks. Hephaestus is good at so many things. He's added this and tweaked that, and the rust is more for show than due to neglect.

Hecate has an image to keep, but she also has grown weary of swallowing Artemis's dust.

They pull into the roadhouse together, and back their bikes in, just two more to add to the line in front of the place. Selene's stands out like it's a pretty-princess bicycle. She has pink fringe hanging from the handles, the bike itself is purple and turquoise, and two doves are nesting on the seat.

"Well, at least she left the swans and peacocks at home, this time," Hecate says as she dismounts.

Artemis's owl swoops down, and Hecate makes no move to stop it from getting the doves. The owl nearly gets close enough to grab them when a bubble of energy erupts up, making the owl scream and flee. Selene must have finally learned not to leave her creatures unprotected.

"That's my favorite owl."

"Teach it better manners, then." Hecate pushes open the door and is assailed by the mixed odors of sweaty humans, beer, vomit, cigarette smoke, and raw fertility goddess on the prowl.

"This place is so disgusting." Artemis strides past Hecate, leaving the scents of pine, bonfires, and new leather in her wake.

Hecate is sure her odor is not so pleasant. Dust and sage and stagnant water. She's long ago accepted it. Selene will wrinkle her nose as soon as she sees her.

Which she does, sooner than Hecate expects, as Artemis yanks her from on top of some rather tubby man in a t-shirt that says, *Heavily Armed,*

Easily Pissed. As looks go in here, Hecate thinks Selene is scraping the bottom of the barrel, but who knows how long she's been here or how much of the barrel she's already scraped.

"We're leaving," Artemis says.

"Call me," Selene yells back to the men, and a few women, who all look ready for a fight.

"You sure you want to leave?" One of the men is reaching for something, and Hecate puts a forgetting spell on him and the others before Artemis can reach for her arrows. It's much easier than bringing Selene's conquests back to life after Artemis perforates them.

"You have no standards," Artemis says, yanking Selene out to her bike. "And your doves should be dead."

Selene smiles and shrugs prettily, then she stretches, the sensual move of a woman in full sexual ripeness. "Those guys were nice."

"What were their names?" Artemis asks. "Give me one of their names."

"Ummm, Tom?" Selene laughs. "Dick? Harry — very hairy, did you see his back?" She shoos the doves off her bike and takes a deep breath of the night air. "I'm in the mood for a ride."

"Do you have to dress that way?"

"Give it time, toots. You'll be dressing this way, too, someday." Selene stretches again, every move making her pink sequined mini dress, with the cutouts just shy of very naughty places, move like snakeskin. She has on matching pink stiletto mini boots. "Where to, girls?"

Hecate smiles. "The north. Where else?"

"You sure we can't have just one more drink?"

Artemis revs up again. "She's sure. Come on."

She takes off, clearly not in the mood for a ride with her sisters to mean actually getting anywhere near her siblings.

Selene smiles. "I had Hephaestus do the same mods to my bike that you had. He's always so grateful to be touched — Aphrodite doesn't know what she's missing."

Hecate rolls her eyes — Hephaestus does the mods for her out of friendship. She follows Selene out, and they fly down the road, leaning into the curves, following the spec that is Artemis. A spec that grows bigger and bigger until they catch up with her and ride three abreast where they can, one of them taking the lead if they see a car approaching.

Artemis glances over at Hecate and says something. It sounds like "Where have you been all my life?"

"What?"

"Who did the mods on your bike?"

Hecate just smiles and shrugs prettily — well, not as prettily as Selene, but she's sure Artemis gets the message that she's not going to out her source. She also knows that for all Selene's I'm-an-open-book whimsy, there's no way she's going to give the secret away either.

Artemis rolls her eyes and guns it.

She only loses them for a moment.

The Girl in the Moonlight

by Gerri Leen

The girl in the moonlight
Dances so freely
Twirling the sun's way
Shaping the pattern
Back to the altar
Building her power
Calling the forces
Wielding her magic
Wherever she touches
Flowers spring forth

The queen in the moonlight
Regally standing
Arms out before her
Singing the secrets
Out to the altar
Starting the passions
Setting her fires
Joyful fruition
Wherever she glances
Abundance is found

The crone in the moonlight
Silently stooping
Calls to all creatures
None can resist her

Come to the altar
Taking within her
All that is living
Healing, transforming
Where once she stood
Now is a girl

Goddess of Pohjola

by Tahni J. Nikitins

It is easy to pass judgment on an old and ugly crone, especially when she is as powerful as myself. The elderly are valued for their wisdom, but often pass before their age gets the better of them. Often they do not see age turn them into shriveled little creatures with sunken eyes and hair so thin as to reveal the shiny, crinkled scalp beneath. I, however, have not yet died, and this is the image of what I am. I am a hunched woman whose skin hangs from her bones. In my old age I still hold great power, just as all elderly men and women retain their wisdom to their dying breath.

I have never denied being a witch, for witch I am. I have never denied conversing with spirits, for converse with them I do. I have more practice in the magic of herbs and midwifery than any other may ever hope to achieve. And for all these things, the men and women of the earth cast suspicious eyes on me and whisper of my wickedness as I pass them by. And even in the light of these things, their hero-men continue to come seeking the hands of my daughters.

My youth has passed, and passed so quickly it seems. Though I have overseen so many generations, watched so many heroes rise and fall, watched gods retire, submitting their thrones and powers to more youthful ones. Someday I will do the same, for even I must eventually die.

When the time comes, I will pass my powers to my last remaining daughter, when all the others have married the hero-men who come to sweep them away from me, just as I have passed every ounce of my youth and beauty to them, divided evenly between them.

I try my best to protect my beautiful daughters. I try my best to keep these "heroes" away from them — these men who view them as pretty prizes to be won from me, the great monstrous witch and goddess of sorcery and black magic. These self-proclaimed heroes are little more than whores and tricksters — though there is something to be said for such beings. I, after all, am one.

Even so, these are not the men I want for my daughters, with their skin fair as the snow blanketing the plains. They are so fair as to be translucent, their fine veins flowing as rivers just beneath their snowy skin, ethereal and light. Their fingers are long and tapered and nimble on their spinning wheels, yielding the finest threads of gold and silver. They have all of the same litheness as I in my youth, tall with lean and strong muscles and hair of fine threaded bronze and night sky falling down their graceful curved backs. Their eyes are vibrant blues and greens and violets, bright and rimmed with long dark lashes.

I made for them chairs and mats in the clouds, safe from the wandering men while they sleep, while they spin, and while they pass their days. From these they can look down at the great expanse of Pohjola, and on occasion pluck stars from the sky and skip them across the frozen lakes. They watch the reindeer, the moose and the elk, the wolf and the great ottava as he lumbers on heavy paws across the ice.

But regardless of how fiercely I try, I cannot protect all my daughters forever. When one falls in love with the man seeking her hand, I cannot stay her from leaving Pohjola with him.

And so the ages have moved beneath Pæivæ. I have lost many daughters to these men, and only a few remain with me. My heart has broken all the way through each time one of those men has left here with his pretty prize: one of my beloved daughters.

In my life I've had many, many lovers. Each time one left at last or was captured by death, my heart broke. But how can that compare to wishing my daughter — composed of my flesh, blood, life, and magic — "fare-thee-well," never to be greeted again? These young and most beautiful of women who suckled at my breast, who grew under my care, ate of the food and drank of the water I provided them; whom I taught to spin and weave and who spun and wove beautiful cloaks for me, whom I taught the ways of life and love — how painful to let them go from my home and into the cruel and deceitful and filth-ridden world of men! How I wish I could bring them back to me, but this will never be so.

And so I am left with only a few daughters, and I hold them as tightly as I can without suffocating them. And one by one they will continue to leave.

Until there is the last. And when there is the last, it will become clear to me that it is time for my own retiring. And so I will pass to her the cloaks I wore as a young and powerful sorceress goddess, and I will pass to her the rings of my fingers and necklaces and torques. I will lay my hands upon her shoulders and lay my last kiss upon her brow, and bestow unto her the very last remnants of what I was, and goddess no more shall I be. But she … she will shine with all of the power and all of the mystery and the dark of Pohjola, lit from within as though with the very power of the rippling lights in the night sky. She will wield all the power I wielded and she shall become the goddess Louhi in my place, and at long last I will travel through the whorl of the spinning sky dome and pass into Tuonela, and there I shall lay in the first restful and deepest sleep of my life, carefully and gently entwined in its depths as though cocooned in the softest spider's silk. I will leave to my last daughter the beautiful Pohjola, which all the men and women fear — this great land of ice and snow and dancing night skies.

❖57❖

[Editor's Note: Originally published in *Eternal Haunted Summer,* Spring 2010]

<u>Greatest (x3)</u>

by Rebecca Buchanan

Thrice-Greatest,
I am called.
And though none
know my true
name, I shall
tell you this
three-times truth:
I am Thoth,
magician
and breaker

of time. The
moon is my
crown and I
record the
wisdom of
the ages,
sharing it
with all who
seek me out.
I am the

most cunning
Hermes, thief,
magician,
and guide of

all souls. I
travel the
worlds, silver
wings quick as
I whisper
eternal

secrets to
those who will
hear. I am
Thoth-Hermes,
silver-beaked,
silver-tongued,
serpentine
staff in one
hand, scroll of
aeons in

the other.
We are all.

<u>Hecate</u>

by Lee Clark Zumpe

Now,
Her cherished dark realm
Subjugated,
Tamed by the devices of technology,
I wonder what ever happened
To poor Hecate.

Now,
As dusk comes shivering
About the concrete towers.
As florescent luster
Pours presumptuously
From glassy-eyed windows,
Overwhelming the starry sky.
As street lamps shepherd shadows
Into secluded alleys.
As twilight cowers before
Apathetic headlights,
And neon and laser luminosity.
Now.

Now,
I find remnants of the dark realm.
Hecate still attends the night,
Lingering on lonely tombs,
At the crossing of two desolate roads,

Or near the blood of murdered men.

Hecate (Detail from Jupiter and Semele)
by Gustave Moreau

<u>Hecate's Domain</u>

by Gerri Leen

Up ahead lies the crossing place
Dusty and lonely
Given over to things that crawl and slither
Rattlers and copperheads, scorpions and centipedes
Hecate's children
Counting off by two

Crossroads dust masks broken
People kneeling at
The intersection of roads
Making promises they won't
Want to keep to a goddess
Older than they know

Hecate hovers — there
On the stop sign
Lounging on the traffic signal
Go
Stop
Slow down — the most important
Consider what you can afford to pay

She won't linger
So many crossroads supplicants
Only one goddess
Snakes dance goodbye

A bobcat stands frozen like a rabbit
By the dark abyss of her eyes

Crone
Witch
Wise One
Dealmaker
She is all and none of these
She flies on, crows and owls at her side
Ancient enemies except
When they attend their mistress
At the crossroads
Real and imagined

Hekate Song

by Todd Jackson

There'll be that in me that yet survives.
I will not lie cold and still without remark.
Someone severs Soul from Bone with knives.

Though it would suffice to feed what thrives
I discern a faint, persistent spark.
There'll be that in me that yet survives.

As a mass of buzzing stirs in hives,
Birdsong waits implicit in the lark.
Someone severs Soul from Bone with knives.

Watching Intellect She then connives
To repeat that Image with Her mark.
There'll be that in me that yet survives.

She repeats the shape of Mind in countless lives,
Then returns them to Herself when each goes dark.
She who severs Soul from bones with knives.

Sure as Ten's division in two Fives
Sure as iron dropped in sand will leave its mark
There'll be that in me that yet survives.
She will slice my Soul from Bone with knives.

Hodh

by Shirl Sazynski

Introduction

I am the only living person who knows this tale, so I am telling it, now. Myths are living things, with pulsing hearts of their own.

Sometimes, when you walk with a God for long enough, you live them out.

Other times — if you're luckier —you enter them in vision.

Believe this, for it is true: when the images begin to dance in your mind, when the characters begin to speak back as you read an old sacred book, it's not always **just** your imagination ….

***

"I know you can't see it now, but I'm doing the right thing," my uncle Loki whispered to me as he put the spear Mistletoe into my outstretched, sweating hand.

Not, "You'll be fine, Hodh."

Trust him to make a joke while my knees were shaking. I prayed the rest of the tribe couldn't see that.

Only warriors perform this rite.

Well, I'm not a warrior.

I was born blind. Some say it was the price my mother paid for bearing such a perfect son, the ultimate son, before me. All of her power was spent in making him, so much poured into it that it could not stay in one body; the weaknesses had to be given birth, too, grasping his heels and squalling red-faced for both of us, all of them rushing into tiny, unexpected, extra me.

Outside the tribe, no one believes that I am blind; how can a blind girl see the other worlds and describe them so clearly? Maybe she blinded herself to see, they whisper. Maybe it was a pact, terrible, unspoken, with the elder powers, great-grandfather Ymir whose mammoth bones lay strewn across the fields and land long before human tongues shaped words, human minds shaped thought. A spine for a ridge, a tooth for a boulder. Hairs that grew up into spiny gorse, thistles, heather.

No, I was born with two very dead eyes, despite all the hawk's blood and a river of ointments, the fervent chants and singing and weeping that my mother applied. It's my soul that can see perfectly fine.

When it takes too long for me to blink, that's when they realize that these two pretty little gems might as well be amber mirrors set into my face.

It's weird for me to see my own staring eyes, so I don't look.

Fearing my power to see all that is hidden, the tribe called me Hodh, Ignorant — as if that could ward off what I might discover.

I am more my father's child. Isn't that strange? My father, greatest of fathers, greatest of warriors, did not begin his life as a king. Nor even chieftain to any of the mortal peoples who cross the great, waving plains of water and grass. His parents were mountain folk.

Which is why I'm doing this.

You move by sound, by temperature, by feel when your eyes can't see. My feet have as much feeling in them as any God's fingertips.

Between me and my perfect brother Baldr stands a pit more profound than the trench the women carved across the initiation ring this morning, a gash crossed only by a single, slender felled oak trunk, its bark shaven smooth off, the green sap cracking from the heat of the smoldering coals below. The spear is blunted so I can't hurt myself or Baldr while trying to cross that trench. Most of the lads stumble at least once before they become adults.

Everyone is blindfolded for this rite. Even flawed, girl me, sweating beneath it, uselessly. But the coals are added to confuse and scare me — the noise, the heat —

How can I sense my brother's breathing, feel the vibration of him touching the ground?

***

Why is she doing this?

All my life, I've seen my sister struggling under the shadow I've cast. No, she is my shadow, born trailing behind me, crying loud enough for both of us —

How many times have we heard that tired story, how my sister was cursed — but if she was cursed, it was only that I'm her brother.

How the fuck did Uncle talk me into this?! It's humiliating for both of us!

It could have been any other warrior who stood for her initiation!

Only the best will do for the King's child. Did your own father not stand for you?

And I nearly failed, uncle.

Yes.

Hodh will fall into the pit. Or crack her bones on the spear tip. One misstep — And I'll see it coming from a thousand long watches away —

Knock her out. A mercy.

When she comes close, tap her across the skull —

***

My father has two children, two twin heirs. Let the tribe not forget: Hodh Odinsdaughter and Baldr Friggsson. We entered this world as one.

All of them are watching me, gathered in a circle wound tightly around us both. Drumming and singing assails me.

I take a deep breath.

When I put my foot on the slender trunk, it bends — down, wobbling — father! don't let me fall, don't let me fail — run with it! — my feet fly across that wavering river of wood, lost beneath the drumbeats —

Solid ground, so hard and so fast that I stumble —

Flailing, blunt spear thrust down into the earth, blocking my fall, but I'm still —

Just touch him with the spear before you fall, my uncle whispered. That's all you need. He's overconfident. He won't guard well.

The blindfold flies off of me as my body swings, losing my footing, throwing everything I've got into one motion —

One chance —

Casting the spear toward the near and waiting silence of my brother Baldr, I pray that it touches him before I meet the ground.

I pray I don't miss ….

And I don't!

High and beautiful, I barely hear the women's singing swell and rise like a tide above the ringing in my skull, the pain of all my spine jarring, my teeth cracking together and all the breath knocked out of me as I collide with the earth in my fall.

In my soul's eye, in a moment that hangs suspended forever outside of time, I see my perfect brother's stony face. Baldr's face, so wonderfully stunned and gaping, and I grin in triumph, as I roll back onto my feet.

And then, strangely, woven through the singing, a scream, pierces the tribal ring.

… Mother …?

I don't … understand.

Why aren't you …?

And then I feel the splinters sink into my palm, the broken piece of ash wood shaft jutting from the back of his chest as I embrace him, the other half lodged in the earth where the spear first sank into it, far too late.

Conclusion

I asked Gerda why she showed me this, when I could think as myself again.

She smiled slightly, to comfort me, because I was alarmed.

"Sometimes you need to know the impossible **is** possible. There is more than one version of this story — there is also this, the secret one the women used to tell."

Yes, this really happened. To me. The rest of the details are woven poetry.

Years later, I entered a Hindu temple, the only one of its kind in the US. It's an odd quirk of fate how I ended up there. Curious, for I had never heard of its God, I pulled up and walked in.

Though the priest had just finished up, and walked out just after I came in, the temple happened to still be open. Graciously, the people inside showed me around and spoke with me.

The temple is dedicated to a little-known God of Doing of the Impossible: Murugan, son of Shiva and Parvati, brother of Ganesh. As far as I understood what the surprised temple-goers told me (they don't get many white visitors), you go to Murugan when you need confidence in the face of insurmountable difficulties. Considered the God of War, among other things, his icon in India frequently shows him holding a spear. Like the Norse God Tyr, associated with both war and justice, his holy day is Tuesday and he is linked with the stars.

According to Murugan's myth, he was born to kill an apparently immortal demon, a being once given a boon by Shiva who then ran amok and terrified both mortals and Gods alike.

Unlike the usual, familiar Snorri Sturleson version that paints Loki as an evil murderer and Baldr as the God of unparalleled goodness, Murugan's myth is eerily closer to Saxo Grammaticus' tale in which Baldr is no innocent, but an unstoppable foe, killed by a human defending both his life and his fiancée from a "forced marriage" (i.e. rape).

The Tamil folk at that temple were intrigued by the Norse tales of Baldr — and completely unsurprised by two contradictory stories with the same motifs within our own mythology (they don't always take theirs so literally). Nor did it particularly shock them that two peoples, separated by thousands of miles, might tell the same tale, greatly altered by time and distance. There is, after all, some **very** ancient history connecting us.

So, which story is true?

Both and neither.

It all depends on who needs to hear it.

<u>Hymn to Freyja VI</u>

by Rebecca Buchanan

the falcon
cloak: i wonder does
it weigh heavy on
your shoulders?

Hymn to Hekate II

by Rebecca Buchanan

she wandered the wild hills and deserts
of Earth's first morning
gathering newborn herbs
nettles petals and leaves
from a boulder
she carved the first cauldron
filled it with the rich waters of Ocean
that crashed beneath her cave
warmed it with fire born of lightning
stirred the potion
bitter strong and sweet
with the branch of a yew tree
dipped a cup deep
and tasted immortality

Enki
by Samuel David

I, Adapa

by Samuel David

al-Minya

The man sat silently, sipping what was left of his tea as he watched passersby in the bazaar. He had already spent most of the week sifting through sand and the remains of another recent archeological dig several miles south in Tell El-Amarna. It was an area for which he had a great sense of fondness and one he now frequented often.

Among the numerous Egyptian artifacts that were found and laboriously catalogued were fragments of cuneiform tablets, largely incomplete and at present indecipherable to the untrained eye. His eyes, however, could discern the meaning of the curious wedge-shaped marks, some smaller than grains of rice on clay tablets little more than a few inches in size. It was not uncommon for out of place artifacts to be found. Empires rise and fall; people become displaced or worse; goods are exchanged, sold, or stolen.

Nothing has changed.

He had somewhat of a following already as a reclusive expert in antiquities with several published papers to his credit that were circulated among a handful of various academics. He was amiable enough many would say, but was often described as rather distant. Even his colleagues could say little else about him beyond their professional relationship. Gossip had spread that he fled Iraq after he and several of his colleagues were targeted by extremists. Some would argue that it was his family — the details seemed hazy. Most, however, preferred not to discuss the matter further.

Some of the gossip was true, to an extent — he did leave Iraq — but he chose not to indulge anyone who would ask.

If anyone saw him in the shade of the canopy erected by the shop owner, they would have given him little thought. His discarded, rumpled tan jacket, wrinkled white Oxford shirt, worn khaki trousers, and sensible shoes allowed him to blend in with the painted walls and wooden furniture. He wore his hat low enough so that no one could see which way he aimed his gaze.

His chameleon-like ability to blend in anywhere came to him over time and he seemed to have had enough time to master this art. He was informed by another in passing that anyone who managed to live beyond one hundred years should have the sense to learn to pass through a crowd without so much as turning a head. He turned few heads now. He could pass for forty now, perhaps fifty. He wore his hair short and shaved his face frequently. Most long-lived individuals he encountered, however, weren't concerned about blending in — some even preferred to be seen, and heard, or worse: proclaim their longevity to all who would hear them.

He spied American tourists who stood out in the crowd, pointing wide-eyed at everything that caught their attention and talking excitedly amongst themselves.

He narrowed his eyes as he saw the street thieves who tried unsuccessfully to keep pace with them.

He caught sight of a young, visibly tired Catholic priest accompanied by several elderly nuns. The young man shook his head in exasperation as he haggled over the price of a bolt of fabric in broken Arabic. The nuns attempted to suppress their laughter as they exchanged knowing glances and then hid their mouths with their hands to prevent themselves from laughing aloud.

Screaming children bustled past them all while waving their arms as a warning. They shouted aloud, *"'Arkad bishakl 'asrae! 'Arkad bishakl 'asrae!"* "Run faster! Run faster!"

The small cup of tea the man held in his hands could be sipped from no more and nothing remained but the black fragments of tea leaves. For a moment, he amused himself with the notion of turning the cup over on its plate to ponder the shapes left by the ground leaves, a form of divination he learned only a few years ago from a shy waiter who sought to impress him.

Reading tea leaves seemed simple — they didn't require the delicate attention to detail of inspecting the livers and entrails he once read long ago to discern the divine will of Heaven. They didn't require the sometimes tedious task of inspection before the ram was sung to and consecrated to the gods:

"O lamb who was born in the field;
O lamb who was nursed by his mother;
O lamb who was called for this purpose.

O ram, you are called by name;
O ram, your name is known by the gods;
O ram, the gods have decreed for you a good fate…"

The most complicated thing about tea was choosing the perfect blend — no one could ever confirm the best tea to use for divination purposes. Even the shy waiter couldn't answer when pressed for one. Was it Earl Grey? Oolong? Perhaps it was a custom blend that shops sold for exorbitant prices to clueless buyers. He'd run into a few of those and always laughed heartily when told the price per ounce or pound before turning and walking away shaking his head.

Choosing the perfect sheep, however, was much simpler — it was to be healthy, without spot or blemish; clean eyes, nose, and mouth. Firm muscles, and a suitable amount of fat.

Some found it necessary to make sure that in addition to appearance and health, the sheep's voice was also perfect by giving the tail or ear a firm tug. The undiscerning would have taken this as a legitimate practice to ensure worth and would gladly pay a higher price. This, of course, was frowned upon and it was not uncommon for a priest or two to box the ears of anyone who found it acceptable to mistreat a ram, ewe, or lamb chosen by the gods for a noble purpose.

Even if the tugging was in jest.

He recalled those among the villagers living near the temple complex who prided themselves in raising sheep as white as the clouds in the firmament of Heaven. Their wool was prized and try as they might, no one could get their shepherds to part with so much as a pregnant ewe to start a flock of their own. Not even the dubious members of the house of Ea-Nasir could make an offer — not that anyone would take them seriously.

His momentary nostalgia came to an abrupt end when a bright light in the crowd startled him. He moved back in his chair as his teacup was jostled from the saucer. As it rolled across the table, the leaves tumbled onto the tablecloth and formed a silhouette of what appeared to be a goat.

He immediately gathered up his rumpled coat, adjusted his hat, and disappeared into the crowd.

Adapa

"In the beginning there was Adapa: chief among men in Eridu;
In the beginning there was Adapa: his word was like the divine utterance of An, the highest of Heaven;
In the beginning there was Adapa: Nudimmud, who is Enki and Ea, gave him a vast and all-knowing mind..."

The boatman punted his vessel across the surface of the sea, pausing occasionally to look at the great city behind him.

The wind was still and save for the call of a lone gull, there was no other sound as he secured his oar, lowered his sail, and gathered up his net. He preferred fishing to replenish the temple's food stores in the cool evening air with his son. They could fish in peace after the other fisherman had returned to shore with full nets and tales of the great fish that still eluded capture despite their prayers and offerings to the gods of the deep.

His heavy net took on a life of its own in his hands and with a flick of his wrist, it appeared to cast itself onto the surface of the water before sinking into the sea. He spoke aloud, addressing the water and the fish beneath its surface, and as he continued speaking, his cadence began to sound like song. His son stood silently with his hands clasped to his chest while his father sang:

"By the divine word of Heaven:
Rise up, O fish!
By the divine word of Heaven, I call you;
Rise up, O fish from the depths!
By the divine word of Heaven, I command you;
Rise up, O fish, fill these nets blessed by the gods of Heaven!
Rise up, O fish, fill these nets blessed by the gods of the earth and under the earth!
Rise up, O fish, fill these nets blessed by the gods of the life-giving sea!"

He tugged the line of his net occasionally and then whispered over handfuls of bread crumbs and barley seeds before he threw them into the water. The still surface slowly began to churn as numerous fish rose up to consume the crumbs and seeds. Within a few moments, the net was filled with the choicest of fish of various sizes and colors. A few who didn't get caught up in the net quickly swam away after eating their fill of the food thrown into the water.

He and his son began to haul the heavy net onto the boat and as they did, the unmistakable sound of rumbling thunder could be heard from the south.

His son shouted aloud and pointed to a looming thunderhead.

Together they fastened the rope of the net to the port of the boat and hoisted the sail, hoping to move quickly to shore. The wind filled their sail and propelled them forward over choppy waves. The mast began to shift under the force of the wind and groaned before it cracked. The thunder grew louder and lightning could be seen in the distance. The boat rocked to and fro. The great cloud moved over them as another gust of wind toppled the mast. The sail whipped back and forth, flapping in the wind like a broken wing. Wave after wave beat against the boat. His son turned to see a larger wave rising up behind them that launched their boat forward and plunged it underwater. In the ensuing panic, father and son reached for each other's hands, but it was too late. The net broke free and caught the young man in its embrace. He kicked and thrust his arms, but couldn't escape. Once, twice, three times, his arms broke the surface, but each time, the net dragged him deeper. His father swam to where he last saw his son's arm breach the waves, but try as he may, he knew his son was lost to him.

He grasped the overturned boat and cried his son's name aloud as he beat his fists against the wood and reeds and pitch that formed the now broken vessel.

He turned his eyes to Heaven and cried out:

"I call upon Heaven as my witness! I call upon the sea as my witness! I call upon the spirit of my son as my witness!

Woe to you, O South Wind! Woe to your form and might! Woe to the wings that carry you to and fro upon the earth and sea!

I curse you, wind! I curse your might! And I curse your wings! I call you fettered! I call you bound! I call you broken!

Hear me and know: I, Adapa, speak these words! I, Adapa, utter this secret spell! I, Adapa, issue this decree!

May the words that I speak be propitious!"

Thunder boomed loudly overhead and the clouds flashed with lightning that spread out across the sky. The wind ceased and the sea grew still. There was no sound and, as he looked to shore, he watched the clouds dissipate over the city.

al-Minya

The man's grey suit appeared to shimmer in the city light as though it were woven from minute strands of silver. His blue eyes looked upon everything he passed, and his hands skimmed the surface of the walls and gates. He was quite out of place as he carried himself with a dignified air. His wavy black hair seemed to move as though it had a life of its own, and his well-oiled beard, like his suit, captured the nighttime lights. His dark skin appeared to be flawless, with no sign of age. No lines graced his forehead, his well-defined brow, his eyes, or the sides of his mouth. His uncanny features were too perfect to be human.

His companion's features resembled his own though he wore darker clothing and a hooded shirt.

The two men walked in tandem, pausing occasionally in the city streets as though listening for something they alone could hear or see or detect with a myriad of other senses.

Hours ago, they walked through a noisy, crowded bazaar full of tourists, locals, and raucous children. Now the streets were relatively quiet save for the occasional sounds of passing vehicles and people talking amongst themselves.

"How long shall we continue our search?" the hooded man said softly as they walked along the city street.

"Is it a search? I see it as a game — and you know how much I enjoy games," his companion responded wryly as he stretched and leaned back against a crumbling wall.

"Yes, although some games don't go in your favor," the hooded man replied. "Drinking games for one, come to mind."

"You forget that even a losing game is a game well-played. This game is, how they say, still afoot," the other said with a smile.

"Ah, yes. Sherlock, is it?"

"And that, my two-faced friend, would make you my Watson."

Adapa

The South Wind hadn't blown from the sea since the death of his son.

His limp body was recovered by the local fishermen and ceremoniously carried to his father's house.

Adapa didn't want the elaborate funeral recommended by the priests of the temple. He wanted his son buried within the walls of the household courtyard.

The wailing procession ended at the gate of his home.

Dressed in linen garments and placed into a reed basket, he was buried near the foundation of the house with his grandfather, his great grandfather and grandmother, his mother and his sister — both of whom died during childbirth. His brothers and sister placed his grave goods in his arms: sealed jugs with water, beer, wine, bread, dates, and fish to keep him from thirst and hunger on his journey to the Underworld. Among the food, they placed jewelry and precious stones as offerings for the Lady of the Great Earth.

Adapa stood silently with a local priest who poured out libations to the gods of the Underworld and prayed for the departed's safety as he passed through the seven gates. He prayed for his spirit to be brave as he stood before the throne of the Lady of the Great Earth where his ancestors would gather to meet him.

Without the wind, the cool sea air could not blow over the land of Eridu and the regions beyond; the crops struggled to stand tall in the dry soil; the people groaned in the heat both day and night.

In the heights of Heaven beyond human sight, An sat upon his throne. He spoke aloud and called his vizier before him.

"Ilabrat, the South Wind has ceased to blow upon the face of the earth and the people's cries of anguish have reached my ears."

"Yes, An," Ilabrat replied. "The wings of the South Wind have been bound and broken by Adapa. He lies sick with despair and fears that he will never fly again. This Adapa, the one who wounded him, is not counted among the gods, but his word is as divine as your own. Everything he utters comes to pass; everything he knows he has learned as one of the Sons of Ea.

"Nudimmud," An said aloud as he bit his lip and struck his thigh. "Very well. Send word to my son that this man, Adapa, is to stand before me and give an account for his deeds."

Ilabrat bowed low and walked to the edge of the garden which surrounded the halls of Heaven. Far below him, past galaxies, asteroids, moons, and planets he could see the earth and its deep sea. He leapt from the edge and flew through the void of space. Within a matter of moments, he stood before the gates of the Apsû, wherein dwelt Nudimmud, who is Enki and Ea.

Enki sat upon his dais in the halls beneath the sea and listened as Ilabrat told him of An's request. His face remained unchanged and his voice did not betray him despite the distress he felt in his heart. He stood from his chair and walked the length of his hall in silence with Ilabrat at his side.

"I shall go to Adapa. I shall instruct him in the ways of Heaven and see that he stands before my father to give an account of my deeds. Tell my father that Adapa will stand before him in three days."

Ilabrat nodded his head in agreement and vanished from Enki's domain.

Enki turned to his mother, Namma, who heard everything.

"I shall go to Adapa and instruct him to appear before my father's throne. See to it that my throne does not remain empty in my absence. Isimud will attend to you while I am away."

Namma nodded and left his presence. She made her way to his dais and sat upon the throne of the Apsû.

Enki rose up from the deep in the form of a great fish and, as he breached the surface, he took on his holy form again. As he walked upon the surface of the water to the shore, his form decreased in size until he was the height of a tall man. His radiant appearance dimmed and as he moved upon the sand, the gulls overhead grew silent. The fishermen upon the shore turned to see him. Some gave him no thought while others gazed upon him in awe and held their clasped hands to their chest. Enki continued in his way, from the sand of the shore to the dense road of impacted clay and the broad streets of baked bricks. He had no need to ask for directions, for he knew the way to the home of his priest.

The door to Adapa's home was closed and from within, Enki could hear the sound of weeping. He touched the door and then knocked softly. A young woman answered the door; her solemn face was smeared with ash. Her red-rimmed eyes stared at him and when her gaze met his, she was awestruck and stepped back into the courtyard. She held the door open wide and stepped back, bracing herself against the wall. Enki raised his hand in greeting, but did not speak to her. The young woman placed her clasped hands to her chest and then hid her open mouth with her shaking hands.

"You are Adapa's daughter? I have come for your father," Enki said. His voice rang in her ears, followed by the rush of blood from her swiftly beating heart. Her hand pointed to the far corner of the courtyard where Adapa crouched, shrouded in sackcloth.

Ash smeared Adapa's face, also, and lines were formed by tears from his red eyes. His beard and hair were covered in dust. He rocked slowly while hoarsely singing words of a hymn. As he sang, he felt his skin slowly prickle — his hair began to stand on end and a shiver lingered at the nape of his neck before traveling down his spine. His breath quickened, knowing that he was not alone. The presence of a god filled his darkened home.

He turned and uttered a cry of despair. Though Enki's radiance was diminished, it washed over his face like sunlight captured in a rolling wave.

"O my Lord! O god of my fathers," Adapa cried out as he fell before Enki and touched his feet. "My house is as the House of Dust and my son has gone down into its depths. This is no place for a god."

Adapa's surviving sons rushed to the edge of the courtyard to join their sister. They stood in silence and watched as their father spoke directly to the god like a man would speak to a friend. They, too, were filled with the fear that their own father was accustomed to though they themselves would never master it. Until now they had only ever seen their father administer public rites upon the great plaza of Enki's temple and on the holiest of days when his great idol was brought before the people. His physical form and likeness made his idols seem crude in comparison.

"I understand your grief, Adapa. Your son was a novitiate in my house — he too was counted among my own sons," Enki said softly. He placed his hand upon Adapa's shoulder. "I would overturn the Order of Heaven and Earth if I could and restore him to you, but I am now forbidden to do so — even for those who serve me in my house on earth."

Adapa remained silent, save for a long shuddering sigh.

"I have come on greater business, as per my father's decree. Send your children away so that we may speak plainly."

Adapa turned to his sons and daughter and nodded. They bowed low and walked backwards, away from Enki's presence while looking to each other for reassurance with bewildered eyes.

"In your anger over the loss of your son, you have cursed the South Wind. Your words were made manifest and now he lies grieving over his broken wings. The Divine Order has been overturned. An has commanded that you stand before him and account for your deeds. I will instruct you on how to ascend to Heaven and what to say as you pass through its gates but I cannot guarantee what will come to pass. I know you are grieving but you must set your mind on other things. Your journey will be swift but we must prepare you before it is too late. I have given my father my word that you will stand before him in three days and the first day is almost at its end."

"What must I do to prepare?" Adapa said as he steadied himself and stood before Enki who, despite his diminished radiance and power, was still taller than the tallest man.

"Do not bathe yourself. Do not oil your beard. Do not wear fragrant oil in your hair. Do not wear your priestly garments. Remain clad in sackcloth and ashes — may the dust be a circlet upon your brow. Go as one in mourning — but not as one mourning his beloved son's death. Instead let your tears be tears of grief for the gods who have left the land for a time. Grieve instead for my son, Dumuzi, and for his comrade, Ningishzida, both of whom stand before the gates of Heaven.

"When they say *'why do you grieve, Adapa?'* you will tell them, *'I grieve for the beloved gods who have disappeared from the earth.'* Do not let your face betray you when you gaze upon them. When they hear your words and see your humility, they will send a favorable word to the halls of An and bring you before him.

"They will extend the hospitality of Heaven to you and offer you food and drink. Do not be fooled, for the food of the gods is not the food of men! If you consume the food and the libations of the gods brought before you, you will take death itself into your body and will immediately descend into the House of Dust to be judged before the throne of Ereshkigal.

"Now, put your house into order. I do not know how long my father will keep you in his halls.

"Give instructions to your sons to go to the priests of my temple — to tell them you must depart. Do not tell them what business draws you away but if pressed, say you are bound by an oath to the gods and swear by my name.

"Give your daughter charge over the household shrine, to offer up prayers to your personal god and goddess in your stead.

"When your sons return, leave your home and come to the edge of the sea. Speak to no one on your journey. I will meet you by the time Utu drives his chariot to the gates of the western horizon. Once you have joined me I will show you the way to my father's hall.

"I will go now and leave you to your children and to your rest."

With those words, Enki vanished like mist.

Immortals, like humans, thrive when their life has purpose. Even those closest to godhood could stave off the slow march of idle despair when engaged with the world around them. Some immortals devote their endless lives to art restoration; some to the exploration of the earth, the Heavens, the depths of the ocean; some to amassing wealth, extravagant wardrobes, and granting interviews to gumshoe reporters.

Some dedicate their lives to living in hiding.

When Babylon was conquered by the forces of Kourosh the Persian, King of the Four Corners of the World, the few remaining Sons of Ea stole away from the holy temple and fled the Place of the Noble Lords.

In the secret hours of the night when all but the night watchmen slept, Adapa gathered in the temple's garden with select members of the priesthood. In the silence, they gathered up their carefully tended garden, separating stalks and roots and leaves and seed pods that could take root in any soil. The stalks and roots were burned, and the seeds and bitter leaves were hidden in loaves of bread. Together, they crossed the borders of the Land in the guise of weary travelers.

Others would come after the Persian, including Aléxandros of Macedon, each under the guise of military conquest while seeking immortality for themselves at any cost.

He parted company with his sacred brothers and traveled west, to the Land of the Pharaohs, the others further east to the Kingdoms of the Rising Sun and north to snow-covered mountains, each taking their secrets with them.

Hiding from would-be conquerors seeking immortality wasn't his only reason to leave.

Another was searching for him.

The morning call to prayer woke him. He prepared his bath and set out his clothes as he considered whether or not to depart given the circumstances. He thought of a suspiciously long-lived monk who resided to the south in an old monastery who was long overdue a visit.

Wherever he would go, however, he knew that it was only a matter of time before he would be need to leave again.

He heard a knock at the door of his small hotel room. For a moment he thought against answering it, but did so anyway. The son of the hotel's owner stood in his doorway with a small wreath made of braided reeds.

"Sir, this was left for you. A man said to deliver it to you this morning. He also wanted you to have this," the boy said, handing him the wreath and a small square of clay. It bore the image of a figure flanked by wavy lines and fish.

The man squeezed the clay in his fist and sighed.

"Very well," he said. "Thank you."

Adapa

Enki stood in the waters of the gulf. Gulls sang above him, spiraling down and up from the lazy waves.

"You have come early, Adapa," he said as he walked forward to the shore. With each step, his radiance diminished and he grew shorter in stature. Adapa was silent as he walked forward upon the sand. He was still draped in sackcloth, and dust and ash clung to his skin. He had observed every instruction given to him, his sons had returned from the temple having said everything instructed to say, and his daughter offered up prayers before the household shrine.

"I cannot go with you — I must return to my halls beneath the deep sea. I will, however, give you this." Enki held a small woven wreath made of reeds. "Wear this. It will bind you to me and to the earth, ensuring that you will return when my father eventually dismisses you from his halls. I trust you have remembered all I have said."

Adapa nodded solemnly as he slid his hand through the ring and drew it up to his bicep.

"Now, prepare yourself. You will see what few living men have seen. I will speak the

Command of Heaven and it shall fall down upon you like a wave. You will be drawn up into that wave like a fish caught in the talons of an eagle. Let that wave, let that eagle, carry you up into the heights of Heaven to the lapis gates of my father's halls."

Enki stepped away and walked deeper into the sea. He turned to face Adapa and raised his voice, speaking in a language that Adapa did not know. His voice echoed upon the water and the hills beyond the shore as he spoke the command of Heaven. It was a whisper and a song and a roar all at once. Adapa looked up as all at once it seemed that the firmament of Heaven had fallen upon him. His body was seized by a great force that drew him up. He felt the rush of wind all around him. In moments he was hurled beyond the atmosphere, beyond the moon, distant planets, and stars, and was cast at the foot of the stairs before the gates of Heaven.

The radiance of the halls beyond the gates of Heaven was beyond compare. It's light dwarfed that of the sun and even the moon. The reed ring upon his arm had become a gold band. He drew his garment down over it to keep it from being seen. His eyes adjusted to the brightness — no doubt thanks to the magic he sensed woven into that once ordinary bundle of reeds.

His unsettling journey left him weak and disoriented. He looked down at his feet and to the starry abyss of space. The glass floor beneath his feet was compact like stone and with each step, he seemed to grow stronger.

The gates before him were massive, each appearing to have been carved from lapis and quartz with glittering veins of gold. To the left and to the right stood equally massive lamassu, both of which looked down upon him with heavy-lidded eyes. Their full lips slowly parted, perplexed that a human would be standing before them. The beings pawed the ground beneath them with their glossy hooves and shook their beards while they unfurled their wings. One of them spoke with a bellowing voice in the same unknown language that Enki himself spoke moments before on the shore of the great sea.

Two radiant beings appeared before the gates: Dumuzi and Ningishzida. Both resembling men with bronze skin, short beards, keenly observant eyes, and generous smiles. They, too, exchanged perplexed looks amongst themselves. Adapa remembered what Enki had told him and lowered his shoulders. He thought of his son, cut down in his promising youth like those gods that miraculously stood before him. He thought of the promise, now unfulfilled, that his own son would stand before the gates of Enki's temple in Eridu and administer the sacred rites long after Adapa had passed through the gates that led to the House of

Dust. He stifled a sob and hid his face behind his hands.

Dumuzi stepped forward, smelling of fertile fields and of ripe dates, of flagons of beer and wine. His dark hair appeared to be tousled by the wind. Ningishzida, too, carried these fragrant smells about him, his own hair resembling tiny black serpents with yellow eyes.

"Who are you, man — and why are you here dressed like one in mourning?" Dumuzi said, looking down upon Adapa's grave face.

"I, Adapa, weep for the sons taken in their prime; the beloved ones of the gods who are missing from the earth," Adapa replied. He had no reason for pretense as he shed genuine tears.

"Who are these gods? Do we know them?" Ningishzida said, his soft voice almost a whisper.

"I mourn for the loss of Dumuzi and for Ningishzida like I would for my own son."

The gods looked upon Adapa and tried to stifle their laughter. Dumuzi clasped a great hand upon Adapa's shoulder and ushered him to the gate that Ningishzida held open.

"Come," he said. "We will take you to An. Perhaps he can help you in your time of mourning." This time, they did not stifle their laughter as the gates closed behind them. The lamassu resumed their positions and their vigilant gaze turned to the distant stars.

Adapa remained focused and calm as he was brought before the throne of An. He bowed lower than Dumuzi and Ningishzida and remained on the floor while the gods stood up again.

"Great father," Dumuzi offered. "This man, Adapa, seems to have lost his way."

An waved a dismissing hand.

"Go," he said, with his great, booming voice. "I will attend to him."

Dumuzi and Ningishzida bowed and left An's presence.

An fixed his gaze upon Adapa who stood slowly, his own gaze fixed upon An's feet.

"I know why you are here, Adapa. We may put aside pretenses. You have done what few humans could do. The divine Mandate of Heaven is the order of the universe. To subvert that order will soon have dire consequences. Even a butterfly can affect great change. You, above all, should know these things."

Adapa had by now turned his gaze up to meet An's own. The radiance of Heaven dimmed while An spoke, as though he had taken it all into his very being. Adapa knew that An's anger was made manifest though he remained regal and composed.

"You are here to give an account of your deeds before the Heavenly Host. But for now, I will send you with my vizier, Ilabrat. He will make sure you are presentable before them."

Adapa was led to a dimly lit hall. In the center of the long hall was a glowing rectangular pool of water lined in gold and lapis. Attendants stood on both sides of the warm water bearing thick towels and clean garments. They bade Adapa to remove his sackcloth and step into the bath and wash himself. They gave him soapwort and a sea sponge to scrub the dust and ash from his body and a comb to run through his hair. They puzzled over the arm band he wore which to them appeared as a braided wreath of reeds. Adapa insisted upon wearing it while he bathed, taking care not to let it slip from his arm. When he had finished bathing, he stepped up out of the pool. An attendant stepped forward to dry his skin while another combed fragrant oil through his hair.

A third attendant stepped forward with clean garments. Adapa was dressed in robes befitting a prince and was given a gold circlet to wear on his head and beautiful sandals for his once bare feet. He was then ushered down a corridor. The three attendants walked to his left, his right, and before him.

Adapa heard voices far ahead and the sound of laughter and music. His silent attendants led him into a banquet hall lit with tiny balls of light like shining stars. The table was full of foods he could barely describe. When he stepped through the door, the gods grew silent and the musicians stopped playing their music.

An clapped his hands together and extended them, welcoming Adapa into their presence.

"Ah, our guest has joined us at last," he said. The other gods murmured amongst themselves.

Adapa spied Dumuzi and Ningishzida among them. Both cocked their heads and smiled quizzically when their gaze met his.

"Come forward, Adapa. Take your place beside me." The gods continued to speak amongst themselves about the mortal in their presence. An turned to Dumuzi and Ningishzida. "My sons tell me they are mourned by those upon the earth in their absence. Here they are." An chuckled. "As you can see, they are alive and well."

"Great father," Dumuzi said. "We know why Adapa has come. We know it is Enki who has revealed the secrets of Heaven and earth to him. We know it is Enki who has shown him the way to the gates of Heaven. Adapa possesses the knowledge of a god. Let his life be like that of a god."

"May it be as you have said, Dumuzi," An replied. "Let Adapa be brought to our table and eat the food and drink the water of the gods."

Adapa was ushered to An's side by one of his attendants and was seated in a cushioned chair of gold.

"In the meantime, Adapa, tell me what the South Wind has done to be dealt such a blow that you broke his wings?"

Adapa felt his throat constrict and his face flushed. He thought of his son, the overturned boat, the funerary rites. He sighed softly and turned to meet An's gaze. He told him everything — of the need to replenish the store of fish for the temple; the sudden wind and coming storm; the waves that capsized his boat; the death of his son.

As he spoke, one of Adapa's attendants brought a platter of food before him with a jug of clean water. A third attendant followed close behind with a jug of beer and another of wine. All were placed before him. Adapa thanked him for their hospitality and continued speaking to An, telling him of all that had happened.

"What you say is true," An replied. "You must set right what you have done. Say the word so that the South Wind may be made whole and take flight again to blow upon the earth."

Adapa nodded and uttered the words to break his spell. His command echoed through the great dining hall. The gods sat astonished at the power that the voice of the mortal among them commanded. Some appeared to be dismayed while others laughed at a glimpse of the probable future in which men would become like gods.

An and those closest to him, including Dumuzi and Ningishzida, noticed that Adapa had not eaten the food brought before him or drank the water, wine, and beer.

"Tell us," Ningishzida said. "Why do you refuse our hospitality? Are you not hungry or thirsty after your journey to Heaven? Have you taken some vow to fast? Is the food of earth better than the food of the gods?"

"No, my lord," Adapa replied as he eyed the food hungrily. "It is true as you say. Enki, my god, has instructed me on the ways of Heaven and earth. He has given me the wisdom and understanding of a god. He has also instructed me not to eat the food of Heaven or drink the water of Heaven. In doing so, I will take death into myself, for the food of gods is not the food of men. I will honor his word."

The gods laughed aloud and then grew silent when An raised his hands. Dumuzi leaned back into his chair and folded his arms. Ningishzida offered to speak, but An spoke instead.

"You have denied the food of Heaven and the water of Heaven: the food and water of life. To deny them is to deny immortality. You have honored your god's word, but in doing so have played into his very hands. You have stayed long enough, Adapa. The day on earth is almost at its end. If you were to stay here when the chariot of Utu passes through the gates of the west, you will die. Heaven is no place for mortal flesh and blood. I must send you on your way. When my son greets you on the shore of the sea, tell him that I request his presence in my halls. We have much to discuss, him and I. Now, Dumuzi and Ningishzida will lead you to the outer gates of Heaven and prepare you for your descent."

The gods nodded, stood before An and bowed low at the waist. They slowly turned and left the banquet hall to stand just outside of its door.

An looked down at Adapa and smiled.

"I would return your garments to you, but it appears they may have been misplaced by the servants of my house. No matter, the robes you wear suit you. I do not know what mourning is to a human, but if it is as painful as it is to a god, know that it will end soon. Your son was in the service of his god when he died. Be comforted in that knowledge. And know that my daughter far below in the Great Earth has a place at her table for youths and babes who enter her halls."

Adapa nodded and slid from the large chair upon which he sat. He bowed low before An and touched his feet.

Dumuzi and Ningishzida met him at the door and slowly walked down the corridor, a hand on each of Adapa's shoulders. Nothing but silence passed between them until at last they came to the massive gates that stood between the halls of Heaven and the starry expanse of the universe.

"You have spoken well for yourself, Adapa," said Dumuzi. "No mortal has sat in the company of the Host of Heaven. Perhaps none ever will — but that is not for me to know. This I do know: it is appointed for man to have one life, one death, and one burial before he must descend into the House of Dust."

"Even there," Ningishzida said. "Some hope may be found. I, and my brother here, have descended below and have dwelt in the kingdom of our sister. We have sat at her table, have stood at her gate, and have served as her throne-bearer. Perhaps the same honor may be afforded to you."

"For now, little brother, return to Earth," Dumuzi said. He turned and spoke to the great lamassu beside him in the same unknown language he had spoken before. The mighty beast shook its beard and spread its wings. A single feather, shining like a jewel in the sun fell to the crystal clear floor. Dumuzi knelt to retrieve it and walked towards Adapa. "You know the way to Heaven. We will teach you the way to Earth. We know of Enki's ring that you wear which binds you to him. That alone will not return you safely should you plummet through the spheres that separate Heaven from Earth. Take this feather and hold it close to you."

"Keep all that you have seen hidden in your heart," Ningishzida said softly. "We will see you again, in the House of Dust. You will be given a seat of honor at the Great Lady's table. If you choose to share your vision of Heaven, then do so wisely and to those who fear the gods and revere them as you do. Now, you must go. Return to your home far below, Adapa."

Dumuzi struck the glass floor with his foot and spoke the command that echoed across the cosmos like a ringing bell.

Adapa turned to his escorts as he stepped to the bottom stair before the gates of Heaven. He clasped his hands before his chest and bowed low. He held the gleaming feather and fell back gracefully. His heavenly robes flowed about him. He passed the spheres and stars and at once saw the beautiful blue Earth before him. His ascent to Heaven was jarring; his descent to Earth was a waking dream.

He crouched upon the shore of the sea just as the chariot of Utu passed through the gates of the western horizon, leaving streaks of red and orange in the sky behind it.

Enki turned to look at him, his man-sized height still greater than Adapa's own. He walked forward upon the surface of the sea and placed a firm hand upon Adapa's shoulder.

"You have seen my father, face to face, and lived," he said softly. "I am pleased."

Adapa smiled weakly and slid the ring of reeds from his arm and placed it in the folds of his robe as he did with the holy feather of the lamassu that Enki did not see.

"Yes, I live," he replied. "I must be off to my family, my lord, as you must be off to your own. Your father has bid you to come to his halls in

Heaven as I have done, for you have much to discuss."

al-Minya

He held the ring of reeds in his hands, fingering the familiar knots and now smooth edges. He remembered when he first put it on, when his senses were overwhelmed with the sight of the cosmos and of the halls of Heaven. He remembered the terror he felt as he stood before An's throne. He thought he had lost it, this souvenir. He had no recollection of what became of it when he returned to earth.

The bazaar was much quieter on this day than usual. The merchants seemed preoccupied with other matters beyond selling their wares. Even those purchasing goods seemed to have set their attention elsewhere. He knew this was no ordinary stillness. Each person here was under the spell of a god, one in particular who could do anything, including sing a rushing river to sleep. He walked to the old cafe, merely a one room shop, where he purchased a cup of tea.

He sat in the shade of the canopy and watched the slow movements of the people all around him.

In the distance, he noticed a shimmer, like the reflection of sunlight on water.

Today, no spilled tea leaves would herald what he already knew. His time had come and he would accept it now.

A man slowly walked through the crowd which seemed to part to his left and to his right. They gave little thought to him or his hooded companion who walked a few steps behind. Their radiance, to the untrained eye, was mistaken for sunlight from above. To those who knew — to the eyes of an immortal — their radiance was seen for what it truly was: the unmistakable sign of divinity or a god's touch. The man in the tailor-fitted suit smiled widely. His too-perfect white teeth flashed uncannily. This morning he wore sunglasses that hid his brilliant lapis-blue eyes. His hooded companion quickened his pace as they approached the man seated under the shade of the canopy.

"At last," whispered the man. "You have finally found me." He stood now and held his hands before his face and then clasped them to his chest when the others approached. "Enki, *zami. Silim.*" He bowed at the waist and looked down at Enki's sleek leather shoes.

"You have done well for yourself, Adapa," replied Enki. "I see that time has been kind to you — and you've cut your hair and shaved your beard. It suits you."

"Yes," Adapa said. "I have come to accept that it has. All the better to 'blend into the crowd' as some would say." Adapa turned his gaze to the man in the hooded jacket and made the same gestures as he bowed. "Isimud, zami. Silim."

Isimud only nodded in reply.

Enki pulled back the old chair that sat unoccupied beside Adapa. He removed his jacket and sat casually.

"Were I human," he said. "I would say that I could scarcely believe that I would run into you. The world, however, seems to have grown so much smaller." Enki seemed amused with himself as he spoke. His hands busily explored the intricate embroidery work of the worn tablecloth.

A pregnant pause lingered between them. Adapa remained silent as though he anticipated anything and everything to happen all at once.

"Yes," he said. "And smaller still when gods walk upon it."

Enki smiled widely and laughed to himself. He leaned forward and touched Adapa's sleeve. His touch seemed to flood Adapa's being like a cool wave that traveled up his spine.

"Come, Adapa," he said. "Walk with me then, on this small world, away from the crowd."

He left his coat on the table as he stood and began to walk out of from under the canopy. Isimud joined him in stride. Adapa lingered for a moment, puzzling over what may or may not come next. He touched the jacket impulsively. It felt like silk and water and fish scales and any number of smooth things he could think of all at once. He gathered it up and held it in the crook of his arm like some holy relic.

He walked several feet behind, unsure of whether or not it would be wise to quicken his pace. The three of them walked silently through the crowd that moved around them like water.

They walked for what seemed like hours until they came to the bank of the Nile bathed now in the early afternoon sun.

"Do you know how many rivers there are in the world, Adapa?" Enki said. "Each one as wonderful as the last. But none as beautiful as the mighty *Idigna* and *Buranuna*. I know each by name, these rivers. This one, the Nile, was once called by the name of its god, *Hapi*. His priests, too, are scattered upon the earth." Enki seemed lost in thought as he spoke. "I know of rivers that have yet to be found, named, and counted.

"You are like these rivers. Swift and always moving.

"I have searched for you all this time and still you were always two steps ahead of me. Few may outrun me, fewer still could make me their fool. I would rather be Ninhursag's fool, or Inanna's — but not yours.

"My father said it was cruel of me to withhold the gift of the gods from you after I had already given you the secrets of Heaven and Earth. Surely by now you have come to understand that I did what I knew to be best for humanity. If you were to be given the gift of immortality, then it would have to be given to all. It is appointed for men to have but one life — in all your god-given wisdom, you know this is true. Look at what has become of the garden we gave humanity. How much longer will it sustain mortals, let alone those who have cheated death in some manner or another?

"Tell me, my Adapa. I often puzzle over this when you come to mind. How did you acquire the gift of everlasting life for yourself?"

Adapa cleared his throat to speak.

"Gilgamesh isn't the only one to have found Holy Ziusudra," he replied coolly.

Enki was silent.

"Funny that," Adapa continued, emboldened by his frankness. "Holy Ziusudra was someone else who had called you lord, god, even father. He, too, would have gone down to the House of Dust had it not been for another god granting him the gift of everlasting life.

"Answer me this, *Mašengurak*, what did I not do in my service to you that was not good enough? You called me by my name before I was Adapa.

"I served you willingly. I devoted myself to your temple — I devoted myself to you. I even gave you my son."

Enki opened his mouth to speak, but instead said nothing. He looked off into the distance and sighed.

"How many others have pledged themselves to your service and were lost?"

Isimud appeared at Enki's side as Adapa spoke, his eyes perceiving every probable future.

"Some would say I am bitter about the lot that was cast for me. I have had millennia to consider my ways. What you would deny your faithful servants, I will give. Even now the faithful living upon the earth strive to rebuild what has been lost to time and trampled underfoot by one conquering army after another. Our beloved Eridu is no more, but another city somewhere can take its place."

"O Eridu, my Eridu," Enki mused aloud. "How often would I have gathered your children together as a hen gathers her brood under her wings…"

Adapa rested his head in his hands, still clutching the reed ring.

"I have spoken enough," he said softly. "Tell me, what are your intentions, my lord? Am I to be taken again before An's throne? Will I be bound beneath the Apsû to keep Mummu company? Or will I be delivered, long overdue, to the House of Dust?"

"Adapa," Enki said, his voice just above a whisper. "It was not your time. I would not grant you immortality in your grief — and not until your young sons and daughter were secured a future. Had you, but waited until after they were taken into the service of the temple, the king, and into marriage, immortality would have been yours, given to you by my very hands.”

Adapa looked up at his god. The realization he had been wrong for thousands of years pierced his heart.

Enki said nothing and for some time, they sat with no words exchanged between them while Utu’s chariot began the descent to the western horizon. It was almost sunset when Enki broke the silence.

“You have done what mortals have only dared to dream, Adapa.

“You have broken the wings of a god; you have ascended to the halls of Heaven and returned to earth; the command of your voice is as the holy word of An.

“In your name, your followers have cast out demons and have driven away the hand of death.

“You say you are no longer angry, but I know that is not true. Millennia may have passed, but you still have the broken heart of a man who has lost what he loves the most.

“I cannot change that, but I can give you what should have been yours long ago.”

“You would do that,” Adapa said. “Even when I have already taken it for myself?”

“Come now, we both know that you must tend that plant as though it were a child sick with colic and each year, consume its bitter leaves. What will become of you should that plant be lost? That is not the life for you — to tend to a fickle plant.

"What will become of the one who discovers it for what it is and takes it from you?

"Even now, there are those who were once part of my order who have chosen not to tend their once sprawling gardens. Some have abandoned them altogether and have chosen to live out their days before descending into the House of Dust. They have come to understand that tending their garden is meaningless.

"Worse still, know that another war is brewing and will be waged not for the acquisition of oil or for democracy's sake, but for that accursed plant."

Adapa paused briefly and stood still. "Some would say Gilgamesh was a fool to have let it slip through his hands," he whispered. "Perhaps it is as you say and his mistake was a blessing. Even though he no longer walks the earth, he is still known by name as a mighty king — as the son of a god — and is now counted among the judges of the dead below. Like me, he would have been subject to the whims of a master he would come to resent."

"What is it that you resent more after all these years upon the earth, Adapa? That bitter plant or my unwillingness to give you what you deserve?"

Adapa was silent. He was wise and knew the secrets of Heaven and Earth, but even the wisest man can sometimes be a fool.

"I am no god," he said. "Take away my long life and I am still a man — a foolish man."

"Ah, but gods take a special interest in fools," Enki said, almost laughing. "Especially holy fools."

Adapa gazed out upon the waters of the Nile.

"I have already declined the hospitality of Heaven and have turned away the food and water of life that was offered to me," Adapa said. "That way is not open to me now, my lord."

"There are still other ways," Enki replied. "If you wish it."

"I have seen all that the world has to offer, my lord," said Adapa. "I have seen the rise and fall of empires. I have mourned the loss of my family. I have mourned the loss of our beloved city. I now mourn the loss of myself in this game against you that I sought to win."

"Perhaps this is no game after all," the god replied. "We meet at the crossroads of your long life. Whatever direction you choose next is your own."

The plant's leaves glistened in the early morning sun shining through the window. It sprawled in its pot like a low-growing shrub. Tiny buds had already formed. Each would take half a year to blossom and then, before long, form tiny seed pods.

He had tended this one for seventy years now, from one home to another, sometimes smuggled through customs with bribes in hand.

Its leaves truly were bitter.

He remembered the warning given to him by the immortal Ziusudra. He must only consume it once a year and after having done so, must endure the night.

He would writhe in his sleep, his body would tense, and he would experience hallucinations and vivid dreams. Once, he nearly bit off his tongue.

Some who undertook this ritual did not always survive.

In these yearly rituals, he often dreamt of his family standing at his bedside. His wife and their stillborn child, his sons and daughter, his own father and mother, his uncles and aunts, cousins and second cousins, and their fathers and mothers before them. Sometimes his bedroom was crowded with the spirits of the dead. Sometimes the dead were not his own. Sometimes the spirits were not of the dead, but wandering daemons sent forth by some god or another.

Despite the harrowing night, he knew the presence of his ancestors would keep him company.

He thought of their shades dwelling in the House of Dust. If he were to join them, there would be no one left to pour libations in their name or tend their shrine. His living descendants were lost to him now. Those who did honor the spirits of the dead had long since died themselves. To some, the dead had nothing to do with the living. They either sleep in the grave waiting to be woken when he who is the Christ returns or when they all stand before Allah during the Great Judgment of men and djinn alike. To others, the dead have no living memory and cease to exist in one form or another when they breathe their last breath. Others still believed the dead are caught up in an endless cycle of death and rebirth, until they reached enlightenment and ascended to the dwelling of An.

He thought of Enki's promise to him and touched the ring of reeds that sat upon his nightstand next to an alabaster bottle filled with the life-giving waters of the Apsû.

He held a bitter leaf in his hand and for a moment caught a glimpse of grey figures standing in the corner.

He put the leaf down and lay back upon his bed and fell asleep to the whirring sound of the fan overhead.

It would be the first time he would ever sleep soundly through the night.

Author's Notes

The mythological narrative of Adapa adapted for this anthology is based on the translation of the original cuneiform tablet. The story is known as "Adapa and the South Wind" and originates from fragmented tablets from the Library of Ashurbanipal circa 600 BCE and older texts from Tell el-Amarna (south of the modern Egyptian city, al-Minya) circa 1300 BCE.

I have taken notable liberties with the myth's narrative. The original myth does not mention Adapa's family or go into detail about his interactions with the gods other than greeting them at the gate and a brief explanation of his actions.

Within the context of myth, these parts of the narrative could be considered apocryphal.

Adapa, over time, became a figure of great prominence and was invoked during exorcism rites. The exorcist would also conflate themselves with him by speaking the proclamation, "I am Adapa!"

I have purposefully used both Sumerian and Akkadian names when referring to the deities depicted in the story — especially Enki. The Akkadians referred to him as Ea (pronounced

"Yah"). Some Akkadian texts however, also refer to Ea by his Sumerian name. Another name used to refer to Enki is Nudimmud.

The name Mašengurak (š being pronounced "sh") used by Adapa when he greets Enki is not found in Sumerian or Akkadian literature. The name translates to "(He) Goat of the Engur" with Engur meaning "subterranean waters" or "abyss." This name used by Adapa in the story is an honorific title for his god.

The word Silim spoken by Adapa roughly translates as "good health" and is not unlike the words Salaam and Shalom that are used today.

The word Zami can be translated as either "hail" or "praise."

<u>Inside the Circle</u>

by Nick Thompson

Hammer Hallow and make holy this ground.
Above me, below me, seal this circle all around.
Needfire creates fire, Flame kindles flame
Before my Gods, I carry no shame.
Spirits of the North, South, East and West,
Witness this act. Let not my words crest.
Between the realms, a day not a day,
A place not a place, I find my way.

Hail thee Freya! Lady of the Vanir,
Daughter of Njord, Who sheds golden tears.
Your beauty inspires and gives men art.
Queen of Valkyries, Mistress of my heart,
Upon this altar, life's essence I spill.
This stone stains red and your touch I feel.
You calm the storms that rage in my soul.
A gift for a gift, a debt we owe.

Hammer Hallow and make holy this ground.
Above me, below me, open this circle all around.
Inside this circle, it was spoken,
So shall it be,
Never to be broken!

<u>Invocation to Medea</u>

by Hayley Arrington

Medea of Colchis
You priestessed the land of your foremothers
Your blood flows with the blood of the Earth
Beautiful Goddess and Priestess,
bless me, a priestess in kind,
to always do what is right in the eyes of the
           Gods

The Golden Fleece rests around your shoulders
now and forever
Beloved Ancestress,
set the Fleece's mantle upon this priestess's back
that I may strive to honor you
I honor you as the Goddess you are!
Blessed be

<u>Magic of the Magician</u>

by Chelsea Luellon Bolton

So you want to start a Witchcraft tradition
focused on Me.
I am the Goddess of Egypt's magic
Not of Europe or Rome or Greece.
Isis as the Moon Goddess is there,
with Her Beloved Osiris.
That is fine.
Those traditions work well.

But not for Me.
For I am a Solar Goddess.
And My husband is the Lunar God.
My Star is Sopdet.
The night is My cloak with rows of stars
burning as lanterns in the night sky.
This is My time.
I am not the moon here.
I am the Stars.
I am the Star Goddess of Night.
The sun at night is not the moon;
the moon reflects light;
it does not burn alone.
I do, as the Star Goddess
Luminously Bright.
I burn as a multitude of stars.
I hold the dead in My grasp.

This is where the magic comes from.
Heka is the power of the vital force, the *Ka*
and this is passed down through family lineages and
        lines.
I honor My husband who died.
So you must honor Me and the Dead.
And this is the First Step
in becoming the Magician.

My Shrine as a Witch
has an image or statue of Me;
two candles;
a bowl of water and a pitcher;
The two Candles represent the Sun and Star
For I am a Solar Goddess
and a Stellar Goddess as Sopdet and
Ruler of the Stars at Night.
The water represents the Nile and Rain
For the Nile is My Husband as well as Me.
I renew Him with My tears
and I herald the flood with My rising on New Year's
        day.
And My colors as the Magician are blue, sea blues
and blues of the night
And the white or gold of light.
These are the implements on My shrine.
But the tools of the Magician are vast and deep.
Which tradition do you desire?
Which methods fit you well?
These will decide the next step in the training.

Water is the flow of creation and life;
This is Mehet Weret's realm.
I am the Creatrix here.
Nunet.
I am the Goddess of Dawn and the First Light.
I am the Sun and Star in the primeval waters.
This witch is good with Water magic.
Speaking into a cup filled with water and drinking
        it.
Drawing up baths with salt, baking soda, herbs and
        spirit waters.
Cleanse and clean.
These are the tools of the Water Magician.

Fire is the fiercest light.
It consumes and devours.
It enlightens and protects.
As solar and stellar light.
This is where I am the Star Goddess
and the Dark Mother of Magic and Mysteries.
For I reveal them in shadows with candlelight.
This is where I reside
as Sopdet, the Dog Star
as the Lady of Stars,
as an Eye of Ra.
I am the Solar Lioness and the Starry-Coated
        Leopard.
I am a Protector and Avenger
I am the Queen of Sorcery and Lady of Magic
All knowledge and all power is Mine to command.

For I am the Great Magician.
I am Ra's Daughter here for I know His Name.
All Magic is Mine as the Great Sorceress,
who heals ailments and dispels darkness with light.
Fire magic will be done here,
to burning petitions in cauldrons
to anointing candles and burning them down.
Fire magic is the Will of the Magician.

I am the Goddess of the Earth,
I nourish the growth of plants and crops.
Earth Mothers are good with food.
This witch will be good in the kitchen.
She will cook her magic and prepare meals,
that heal or avert harm.
Food and Herbs are My tools here.
Yes, flowers too.
All plants are under My domain.
For I am the Goddess of the Crops.
Adorn My shrine with food offerings
and garlands of roses
for these are My symbols
as the Goddess of the Land
as both Mother and Wife.
And yes, Widow too.
Roses were used to adorn the graves.
Other flowers too.

Air is Breath.

Spoken and written words become more potent
        when read aloud
Magic is in the breath.
Sing songs of My recitations
Sing songs and praise-hymns
And My magic will flow
and I will bestow blessings to those who speak or
        sing of Me.
Poetry and oracles are within this magic.
For words are uttered by the mouth.
Chant and sing the words of magic power.
For this is the magic of the Magician.

All of these elements together make up My magic.
For those who will learn it and seek it out.
Become the Witch
Become the Magician
Become the Sorceress
Become whom you most desire to be.
And that is the Magic of the Magician.

<u>Myrddin</u>

by Lee Clark Zumpe

no other spell-strung legends
like yours from the Dark Ages
linger on the lips of scribes.

some wild Welsh nomad —
barefoot, gaunt, and crude —
possessing keen intuition

or seer, Satan-spawned,
spreading ingenious rumors:
twisting history with intent.

cryptic forces conspired,
aiding the son of Uther,
and your narcissistic goal —

upon you romancers bestowed
the precious gift you craved:
none can deny your immortality.

<u>Nimüe</u>

by Hayley Arrington

They say I locked him far away
In a cave or under a mound.
But do they say what he did to me
Before I put him in the ground?
He weaved his spells to woo me
He went stark raving mad
And yet he did not soothe me
With tales of a far-off land.
I do not know this story you say
I only know my own
And wish you'd only hear my words
Before I turn to stone.
The day was young
The sun had set
The summer air left me cold
He said he'd make me his dear pet
Before the season was old.
I learned the words to change
Winds from west to east
I learned the words to stay a hind
So we could have a feast.
And yet the word I wanted best
Would tear me limb from limb
He put his hand upon my breast,
That word I'd not get from him.
So, maybe he slumbers

Awaiting the day
Of winter's icy reckoning
Or maybe he's dust
Beneath a tree
His eyes no longer beckoning.
And, yet, the word I heard one day
Spoken loudly in my mind.
I said the word aloud myself
And left the world behind.

*["Nimüe" was previously published in **Folk Horror Revival: Corpse Roads** from **Wyrd Harvest Press** in 2016.]*

<u>Nitokris</u>

by Ashley Dioses

Beneath the yawning gateways, underneath the last,
Third Pyramid, the ghoul-queen sleeps within the
      vast,
Nethermost onyx temple, in the void below.
She sleeps amid rich gems, untouched by sunlight's
      glow,
And with the mummies that are neither man nor
      beast.
Still living, she was buried for a deadly feast ….
Some shun her Pyramid beneath Egyptian moons —
Queen Nitokris was legend 'mid the desert dunes.

The great Sixth Dynasty portrayed a nymph in
      youth —
How easily she lured her foes in peace; in truth,
She offered them unto the Nile and drowned them
      all
By throwing wide the water-gates in Temple Hall.
Her cachinnation echoed still as she was thrown
Into her grand sarcophagus of golden stone.
She lies there with Him of the Sphinx, as tales were
      told —

He of the Second Pyramid, Khephren of old.
So far beneath the ground, he wed the ghoulish
queen,

And with her ruled over the mummies, vaguely
      seen.

The horrors Egypt hides endure in olden tombs,
Where phantom priest-processions still disperse the
      fumes
Of richest resins as they offer up their gods
Unspeakable, dread sacrifice impaled on rods.
The mummies without souls and hordes of devil-
      cursed
Pharaonic dead and restless kas know wicked thirst
Amid the onyx darkness of the queen and king.
The queen awaits whatever desert sands may bring.

The stone colossi marched in endless night and
      drove
The herds of grinning androsphinxes down a cove
To shores of stagnant rivers, black as pitch and cold.
It was her necromancy that called through the hold
To lure the dead and servants there so she could
      steal
The spirits out of victims lost and make them kneel
Before her as sweet sacrifices or new slaves.
Yet each new offering would fall unto their graves
If they should merely glimpse her visage, for the
      fools
Would see her face was gnawed by rats and starving
      ghouls.

*[Author's Note: After H.P. Lovecraft's **Under the Pyramids**]*

*["Nitokris" was originally published in **Weird Fiction Review** #7 by **Centipede Press**.]*

*Pyramids of Giza from **Egypt & Nubia**
by David Roberts (1846-1849)*

Orphic Archeology

by Mark J. Mitchell

The oldest attestation for the Bacchic cry euhai! —
comes from Olbia, inscribed on a mirror from a
woman's tomb dating to about 500 BCE.

> —*Walter Burkett,* **Babylon Memphis**
> **Persepolis***, page 84*

Time back: She didn't call the god's real name.
She made a sound he liked. The lake grew hard,
grew smaller. Silvering ice formed a frame.
New born letters arrived. They chose to carve
the sound in something she chose to call glass.
He built her a big house. Built a small room.
She lived forever. It became her tomb.
That hard mirror on her table. Time passed.

Light leaks into an ancient room today.
Dust rises. Mystery frescoes undress
for scholar's eyes. Sunlight dances. It plays
on — something. Blind teachers try to focus
on stiff forms carved in glass. They might shape
her name — a woman, killed by a god's kiss.

2.

Time back she was told — there is a white lake.
Do not name it. Keep it on your left side
and never taste the water. Your path takes

you down a quick slope. It is always light,
there's no darkness to fear. Speak your real name —
not what your mother handed you. The guard
will give you a word you don't know. It's hard
sound will part stones. Through time, this stays the
            same.

Fragmented gold, too brittle to be touched
lies spread on a table. Cold instruments
are poised to decode language. There's not much
there. Lab coats slide on — secular vestments.
Technicians tame their breath, pale faces flushed,
tense before old knowledge. Trembling. Silent.

3.

Time back, she notices — there's no breath here —
not from her mouth, not from animals
who walk past her, brushing not flesh. A deer's
coat's cold, hooves are silent. She can't quite tell
it's passed. She was told to wait for a song
below a white lake. She stands — statue stiff —
listening to absent air. Leaves don't lift
when birds fly up. She'll wait. How long? How
            long?

In a cold room a small woman's white coat
shifts on her shoulders. Her fingers unroll
papyrus. Her pen is poised. She knows notes
must be kept. The script's linear — so old
she shivers to think of the hand that wrote

it out. The room is still. Bright and cold.

4.

Time back: A tree arose at her left side.
Its leaves moved, soundless, singing no soft notes.
His song would come, she prayed. There is no sky
in this cold place. Silver-gold petals float
on that white lake. Guards offer her cool drinks
but she refuses tastes. That means real death,
not this half-waking walk and absent breath
but nights that don't end. Gold leaves start to sink.

The white walls hold rubbings that can't be read —
not yet. Pulled off gravestones, they almost seem
ready to speak but her work-rigid head
fails. When she was a girl, almost, she dreamed
of all the letters unwritten by dead
hands — lovers and priests. Now they're cold
      phonemes.

5.

Time back: She feared the lyre, not the arrows
that thrilled the air — silent, swift and harmless.
She wished out loud for stars, but her heart knows
that music alone will call them out. Her test
is waiting, seeing his famed cap and face
with her mind. Behind her — is that a note?
Low — lyre's fat string. No, an animal's throat
opened. She feels the lake. She's not afraid.

Black coffee beside an open notebook
steams up her glasses. She only wants words
to give up meaning. She takes quick, sly looks
at pages, rubbings. Everything she heard
in school leads to here: A white room, books,
a table, no windows. She misses birds.

6.

Time back she heard the mother of dreams call
her name while leaves sank in still water.
She trembles, fearful she'll give in to small
temptations. She knows she's nights lost daughter.
She must surrender, release honeyed dreams,
listening for his voice, song, his sweet lyre
(and remember that he's still a sweet liar).
So still: She knows she knows what nothing means.

Her eyes fail her daily. Dream residue
clouds work. She's the keeper of catalogs
today only. She knows there's nothing new
to see. She doesn't mind piercing drab fog
but she wants one holy word to break through
so she'll know she's not a machine, a cog.

7.

Time back, her still eyes twitched. She held her
      head
stone stiff and felt — not seeing — a chasm
open to her left. She was new to death,
so arms chilled and a quick, unwilled spasm

traveled her leg. She thought a woman passed
to that long left, wearing something long, white —
a garment she didn't know. Not trusting sight,
she breathed out the holy words she'd heard last.

Somewhere in her room a bell rang a note —
A above Middle C — she saw the script
reflected on a clock face and she wrote
a word she knew — light entered her crypt.
She'd found a backward path into the code.
She sit-jumped. A small song escaped her lips.

8.

Time back — when they were small, they liked to play
   play
with chaos. He would juggle, sing. She laughed
and clapped. She remembered those lost, bright days
   days
standing under a not quite sky. One half
of her face smiled. Then the woman in white
passed again — writing words. The glowing pit
almost swallowed them. Her loose balance slipped.
She thought of his songs and stayed upright.

Something shifted in her white room. Her eyes
lost focus. The bell kept ringing. Her ears
were useless. The notebook was telling lies.
She wanted teachers to come back. Slick fear
slid up her spine, sharp and cold as a knife.
She couldn't move. Her brown eye dropped a tear.

9.

Time back a calmer chaos wrapped her. Birds
lit, forming lines of letters in gray grass.
Her lips opened—shaped wild meters. She heard
what she saw. Her bones thrilled. The lake moved
      past
her body. There was — not light — but motion
in vacant sky. The sounding of six long strings
rang out behind her. She hears — Him. He sings
her names. Now. Time swallows like an ocean.

Her room wasn't white. It moved to half-tones.
Letters leap up into words that she knows
with her small body. A message from stones
opened. The room vanished like a rainbow.
Suddenly, she knew it all in her bones.
Happy and lost — she was ready to go.

10.

Time now — she is born new, fresh-hatched. Her
      shell
in pieces, littering dark earth under sky
that lacks lights — no sun, no stars — if it's hell,
she'll take it. The long white coat molts off by
a loud chasm rimmed with trees near a lake.
And trees dance with flowers, water — with her!
She screams a song with no meaning. White birds
spin through this dream. She doesn't need to wake.

A white room. A circle on a wall. She
spots her face in something clear. She reacts —
careful not to care. She wants to see
beyond this room. His song — its magic acts
on her white soul. Doors give her days. She's free,
breathing. She shouts, "Euhai!" and takes time
            back.

11.
Coda: Words About the God

The god is older than you know. His face
stays smooth but it's built from the broken bones
of earth. Because he draws women with grace
and music, you miss his force. You erase
his murder. He masters death, plays with fate.
His lower word error, that last look, known
to all, reveals secrets—not named, but shown.
So don't mistake his beauty for weakness.
His songs reign—above, below. There's no rest
for him. Women prayed. He played them. Their
            game
pleased vanity. He moved them up or down
for amusement. Women are not ashamed.
It's his will to answer to his real name.
He's an ancient god. He's always found.

by James B. Nicola

A priestess never needed a black cat,
nor, necessarily, a broom to fly,
nor sported warty nose and conic hat;
we have the Modern World to thank for that.
Nor did she ever tout as her ally
the guy with hooves and horns in bright red dress.
It was the Patriarch that made the switch
and changed the awe-some into an abscess,
and what was sacred, into ugliness
herself, the holistic into a witch,
a crone, or at the very least, a crank.
I was not nine yet saw something amiss
in those harsh demonizing ways, and thank
Elizabeth Montgomery for this.

*[Originally published in **Contemporary Rhyme**.]*

The Resting Place

by Gerri Leen

Hecate walks the roads, stopping at
The crossing place
Bats zing overhead
Dancing this way and that after bugs
That never dare bite her
An owl hoots; a colony of crows
Rustles nervously in a nearby tree
Her black beauties would fly
Like the bats if this were day
But it isn't, it's midnight
At the crossroads
And she breathes in the night air
Opens her mouth
And yips like a coyote
All around her, return cries echo

But there, another sound
A car, weaving, going slowly
The driver either tired or drunk
She waits to see which
He brakes before he hits her
Parks crookedly, lying half on
Half off her beautiful cross
His eyes are open, but close
As he slumps, lights on, car running
But not moving — he's put it in park

Doesn't want to hit her
Drunk then, drunk but kind
She moves around to the window
Mortals come to her for favors
Not for rest
That's another god's domain

Yet she can read this one's pain
He's more crow than owl or bat
He should be home, with those
He loves but he's far from them
He's here at the place of wishes
But has none to make
She opens the door and crouches
"What will you give?" she whispers
He answers in a language from the south
Speaks of pride and hard work
And loneliness
Such crushing loneliness
She closes the door, lays her hands
On the roof and sends him to the
Place he sleeps — it's nothing like home
But it's better than this
She tries to pretend this isn't kindness
He was in the way, after all
If someone came to make a deal
Her crows croak in their tree
The coyotes yip a little louder
And the bats continue to hunt
Just another night

At the crossroads

Triple-Bodied Hecate
by John Cosway

<u>Selene</u>

by Gerri Leen

The moon's light shines
Through the crack in my curtains
Falling on my face
I awaken
I feel Her power
Calling me back
Get up. Get up
Come dance with me
The night is warm
The priestess blood within me
Runs slow
Another time, another night
I turn away
Block out her light
But in my dreams
I dance.

The Sleeping Forest

by Rebecca Buchanan

the trees walk in their sleep,
their leaves a quiet rustling,
their roots gentle in the earth,
leaving foxes undisturbed in their dens
and ravens quiescent in their nests

the forest sleeps as the wizard sleeps,
tucked deep in his oaken bed

his robes are still bright,
his beard still neat,
for no wind has blown,
no rain has fallen,
not since the lady
breathed her sigh of sleep

perhaps he dreams

the trees certainly do,
and they walk as they dream

if you would find
this wandering forest,
you must walk, as well

take care, though,
or you will join those others
who have dared to seek the sleeping forest
and now lie among its roots and trunks,
their clothes still bright,
their hair still neat

find the wizard's oaken bed

whisper your question
through the crack in the bark

perhaps, in his sleep,
he will dream a true answer,
and whisper it to you

if you have no question,
take an acorn from among the leaves,
carry it gently home,
and find a spot of rich earth
for it to grow

your dreams will always be true

if you have no question,
and no wish for a tree,
collect a branch,
the right size to fit in your hand

feed the branch clean water
and warm sunlight,
and your spells will always be true

take care, though

be quick and be quiet
as you walk,
for the lady still watches over
her sleeping wizard

if you hear her sigh,
you are already lost,
carried away by the trees
as they sleep and dream

The Spell of the Sorceress Grimhild

by Sarah Yasin

He is mine,
the boy without fear.
Today I carve runes inside
the drinking horn
deep down where eye
cannot see.
Fist-strained I scrape
with needle
as my blade.
None shall sense
the dreg-grave spell.
And when he drinks
my magic ale,
all memory of her
shall fade and vanish away.
Sink down, Brynhild:
he is mine.

<u>Strega</u>

by Nancy Byrne Iannucci

Congregating in scheming circles as ritualists
       surround
a sacrifice, their perspiration anointed my face like
      a baptism.
Fireflies snapped off of smoldering wood stifling
      the old kitchen.

With a tiny shot-glass between garlic clove fingers
yellow liquid snaked my mouth like an unwanted
      tongue.
Stings pierced through their eyes like stabbing
      daggers,
spiraling to examine the effects of their exploit.
Stained glass fragments shattered my sight blind.

~ ~ ~

"Come with me," the crone crooned.
Her crescent moon face turned to guide like Virgil
above the Mediterranean Sea to Monte Mutria
in the province of Benevento.
She pointed
        d
         o
          w
           n

we dropped onto a labyrinth of roots
at the base of an old walnut tree.
Shadows of its branches whispered primordial tales
of my ancestors through each brackish breeze.

Chants of feminine laughter frolicked half-naked
dancing like sybarites before the ancient tree.
Centaurs led the dance then moved towards me
through the Fog —

~ ~ ~

Gathering myself up off of the kitchen floor,
the ferry-women grinned like cats knowing
I had traveled on their token.
"Hai ancora paura della bevanda?" They asked,
        anxiously.
"No, Io non ho paura," I answered with a knowing
        mien.

"Andiamo!" they intoned merrily in operatic form
as they waved their hands in a gruff announcement.
My aunts scuttled to place a mirrored tray
on a worn butcher block table.

A bottle of Strega Liqueur
stood regal atop the mirror as the fairest one of all.
Five shot-glasses surrounded her like ladies-in-
        waiting

for us to return to our roots under the old walnut
tree.

Diana
by Simon Vouet (1637)

<u>Taliesin</u>

by Hayley Arrington

They say I am a bard,
The mightiest of them all,
But I know the real story
When I hear the raven's call.

The winter's winds have lessened
But a drought lays o'er the land.
My lover's eyes have beckoned
From behind a peacock fan.

No more the days are lengthening,
No more the sun shines true;
But nighttime's cries are beckoning
For a heart that's icy and blue.

The stories that I've told before
Are a far cry from the stories I know.
These stories come from within my core,
They come from a land of snow.

So do not assume
That you know my tale
When I've told all I have to tell.
Leave me alone with my stories to dwell
Till my coffin has its last nail
And Death my stories consume.

Villanelle: Odysseus' Afterwords

by Todd Jackson

Darling Circe, leading me to sin.
As I rest my head between your thighs
Whisper me what beast I would've been.

Ichor pulses cool beneath your skin.
By this deathless blood you mesmerize.
Darling Circe, leading me to sin.

Turning sailors into Otherkin.
Some to ursinate, some leonize.
Whisper me what beast I would've been.

Kiss you up and down your eight foot ten.
Let's again before this morning dries.
Darling Circe, leading me to sin.

Would my sweat bead up a dorsal fin?
Does my tongue inspire butterflies?
Whisper me what beast I would've been.

Now again to taste the light within,
Stir your repertoire of little cries.
Darling Circe, leading me to sin.
Whisper me what beast I would've been.

<u>Witching Hour in the Suburbs:</u>
<u>A Devotional Poem to Hekate</u>

by Clarabelle Fields

Hekate, witch-mother, goddess, guide

it's one of those nights when
the sky is kissed with ethereal promise
and the wind itches on your skin and
the scent of damp rain lingers longer
than usual, stars heavy at the brim
of her velveteen hat —

I thought I saw her,
I followed what I thought was a cat
silky dark like a cold ember
through the black night
through sleeping streets
and shuttered houses
with burned out eyes,
gates left off the hinge
just enough to beckon inwards
a silent wisp, a hint of broom-
smoke wafting through
dying trees

I followed her,
I followed her down
corkscrew paths past

libraries with one light left on
and sleeping courtyards and
quiet gardens, past empty echoing
churches at the city's edge, past
the city's fires and out
into the sweet, low-lying prairie
where she crowns her witches
with garlands of frosty flower petals

I followed her,
I followed what I thought was a black cat
black as a raven, black as the ink
that the witch-mother draws from
when she's dyeing the fabric
she weaves for us, breathes for us

Hekate, witch-mother,
I followed you in the darkness
your quick paws shining
obsidian against stars

Hekate, witch-mother,
I followed you, warm in your
shadow, I followed you
in another's robes,
your warmth in my throat, moving
hidden blood in my hands

I thought I could catch you this time
I called out for you, calling your name

Hekate, witch-mother, goddess, guide

I ran after you in the glow of the storm
and you paused long enough
to leap into the air
wings downy and silent
in the black night

somewhere,
a single windchime
is dancing alone in a tree
and I am calling for you
calling for you

Hekate, witch-mother, goddess, guide

<u>Young Circe Discovering Witchcraft</u>

by Clarabelle Fields

I.
moonlit marble cold underfoot
Circe pauses a moment
letting Diana's goodbyes
filter softly into velvet night
a gift comes too, this time,
a basket of fresh stars
still budding, just born
beginning to tremble
with dawning warmth

curious, she lets a newborn star
slip between her fingers
and it spreads into a powder blue arc
singing soft hymns as it falls

II.
ripples over treeheads,
stars flickering briefly
blue to purple to white
she has learned to braid them
and bring them home

III.
smiling,
Circe draws

the cup to her
steam revealing
the heart of a ripe star
pink and purple petals
fading fast
to leave a silver core
shimmering and
spinning
in the tiny buoyant dark
a will, hers,
melting into diamond night

Appendix A: Select Deities and Other Figures

Adapa (Sumerian): He unknowingly(?) refused the gift of immortality. An important figure, his name was used in exorcism rituals. He is the archetypal wise ruler.

Aradia (Italian): Daughter of Diana and Lucifer. A messianic figure and the first witch, she was sent to Earth by her mother to teach magic to the people, that they might free themselves from oppression. An important figure in Stregheria, as well as some sects of Wicca and witchcraft.

Artemis (Greek): Goddess of the hunt, wilderness, moon, chastity, and childbirth. Considered the particular protector of young girls. Widely venerated in the ancient world, she is often linked to **Hecate** and **Selene** as either a Triple Goddess or a triad.

Brigid (Celtic, particularly Irish): Goddess of spring, domesticated flocks, healing, poetry, inspiration, fire, and smithcraft. Possibly a Triple Goddess, possibly a triad of three sisters. Widely honored in contemporary polytheism.

Ceridwen (Welsh): An enchantress/Goddess. Mother of the hideous Morfran and, inadvertently, the bard **Taliesin**. Owner of the cauldron of inspiration and transformation. Popular in contemporary Goddess Spirituality, and among Brythonic polytheists.

Circe (Greek): Goddess of magic and transformation. Daughter of the Sun God Helios. Her mother is sometimes the sea nymph Perse, sometimes the Goddess **Hecate**. By her brother Aeëtes, she is the aunt of **Medea**; and by her sister Pasiphaë, she is the aunt of the Minotaur, Ariadne, and Phaedra. Best known from her appearance in *The Odyssey*, in which she transforms Odysseus' men into swine. Appears frequently in literature and art.

Daoine Sidhe (Celtic, particularly Irish, and Gaelic): Also known as the aos sí, aes sídhe, and daoine sith. A supernatural race comparable to fairies or elves. They are said to live in underground halls, or across the western sea, or in a world parallel to our own.

Diana (Roman): Goddess of the hunt, wilderness, women, childbirth, and the moon. Revered in contemporary Stregheria (see **Aradia**), Wicca, Religio Romana, and other polytheist traditions.

Enki (Sumerian): God of water, wisdom, mischief, magic, crafts, and creation. Also known as Ea. An ancient Deity, worshipped throughout Mesopotamia from approximately 4500 BCE through approximately 550 BCE. A popular God in contemporary Sumerian polytheism.

Freyja (Norse): Goddess of war, death, love, sexuality, beauty, fertility, gold and amber, and seidh (magic). She possesses a cloak of falcon feathers, often transforming into that bird of prey to wander the Nine Worlds.

Gerda (Norse): Goddess of the earth, closely associated with soil and fertility. Also spelled Gerðr. The giant (jotun) wife of the God, Frey.

Grimhild (Norse): A sorceress and queen, wed to the King of Burgundy. In the *Völsunga Saga*, she brews a potion for Sigurd which makes him forget his wife, Brynhild. Another Grimhild, also a sorceress and the wife of the King of Alfheim, appears in *Illuga saga Gríðarfóstra*.

Hecate/Hekate (Greek): Goddess of magic, witchcraft, crossroads, entranceways, boundaries, the underworld, and the night; often associated with the moon, and sometimes a triad with **Artemis** and **Selene**. She appears in numerous works of ancient literature, as well as modern art and literature. Widely worshipped throughout the classical world, and one of the most popular Goddesses among modern witches, Wiccans, and polytheists.

Hermes Trismegistus (Greek, Egyptian, medieval Christian, Islamic, modern occultism): In the classical world, he was a syncretic being combining elements of the Greek Hermes and the Egyptian Thoth, and was believed to be the author of the *Corpus Hermeticum*. Medieval Christian theologians saw him as an astrologer, alchemist, magician, and proto-monotheist. In Islamic tradition, he is equated with the prophet Idris.

Hodh (Norse). Also Höðr or Hodur. In traditional sources, such as *Gylfaginning* and the *Völuspá*, he is the blind son of Odin and Frigg. He slew his brother Baldur with a sprig of mistletoe.

Isis (Egyptian). Goddess of sovereignty, magic, healing, and motherhood, among many other things. Worshipped throughout the ancient world, from roughly 2600 BCE (the first appearance of her name) to roughly 500 CE. One of the most popular Goddesses among modern polytheists.

Louhi (Finnish and Karelian). Possibly an alter ego of the Goddess, Loviatar. Described in the *Kalevala* as a powerful, evil witch queen who is the main antagonist of Väinämöinen. She has a number of beautiful daughters. Louhi sets difficult tasks for the many suitors who come calling.

Medea (Greek). Sorceress, priestess of **Hecate**, and niece of **Circe**. After using magic and herbalism to help Jason steal the golden ram's fleece from her father, she fled with Jason back to his homeland and married him. Years later, he set her aside in favor of a younger woman. Medea's response to this abandonment varies by author, but none of them are pleasant. Her adventures continued, according to both classical and modern authors.

Myrddin (Welsh). Also known as Merlin. Sage, wizard, engineer, and chief advisor to Arthur in the court of Camelot. He is said to be buried (or sleeping) in the forest of Brocéliande, having been placed there by **Nimüe**.

Nimüe (Welsh). The Lady of the Lake. An enchantress who plays a pivotal role in Arthurian lore: she gives the king his sword, raises Lancelot as her son, and bewitches (or is nearly bewitched by) Merlin.

Nitokris (Egyptian). According to legend, she was the last Pharaoh of the Sixth Dynasty. In Herodotus' *Histories*, her brother, the previous Pharaoh, was murdered. Nitokris invited the men responsible to a grand banquet, murdered them all, then committed suicide. Supposedly.

Odysseus (Greek). King of Ithaca. One of the leaders of the campaign against Troy. Husband of Penelope, favorite of Athena, lover of **Circe** and Calypso. Wanderer, liar, thief, soldier, con artist, hero.

Selene (Greek). Goddess of the moon. Sister of Helios, making her the aunt of **Circe** and the great-aunt of **Medea**. Sometimes part of a triad with **Artemis** and **Hecate**.

Taliesin (Welsh). Renowned bard of Camelot. The many tales about him are possibly based on an historical person. In myth and lore, he is a servant of the Goddess, **Ceridwen**; he stirs her cauldron of inspiration for a year, then drinks three drops that splash on his thumb. He gains all of the wisdom of **Ceridwen**'s potion.

Appendix B: Our Contributors

Edward Ahern resumed writing after forty-odd years in foreign intelligence and international sales. He's had over two hundred fifty stories and poems published so far, and five books. Ed works the other side of writing at *Bewildering Stories*, where he sits on the review board and manages a posse of six review editors. He can be found on Twitter at https://twitter.com/bottomstripper and on FaceBook at https://www.facebook.com/EdAhern73/?ref=bookmarks.

Hayley Arrington is a mythologist, poet, and writer. She received her MA in women's spirituality from the Institute of Transpersonal Psychology in Palo Alto, California, where she wrote her thesis on Celtic sun goddesses. Her writings have appeared in various publications online and in print, including *Eternal Haunted Summer*, *Goddess When She Rules: Expressions by Contemporary Women*, *Inanna's Ascent: Reclaiming Female Power*, *Liminality* Magazine, *The Far-Shining One: A Devotional to the Spirits of the Sun*, *Goddess Devotional: A Prayerbook Honoring the Sacred*, and elsewhere. She is a devotee of Pre-Olympian Hera and a priestess in Temple Sophia. Hayley is from the greater Los Angeles area, where she lives with her husband and son. Read her Arthurian Witch blog at loathlylady.wordpress.com.

Chelsea Luellon Bolton has a BA and MA in Religious Studies from the University of South Florida. She is the author of the devotional collections, *Lady of Praise, Lady of Power: Ancient Hymns of the Goddess Aset*; *Queen of the Road: Poetry of the Goddess Aset*; *Magician, Mother and Queen: A Research Paper on the Goddess Aset*; *Lord of Strength and Power: Ancient Hymns for Wepwawet*; *Sun, Star and Desert Sand: Poems for the Egyptian Gods*; *Mother of Magic: Ancient Hymns for Aset*; *Queen of the Hearth: An Anthology for Frigga*; *Flaming Lioness: Ancient Hymns for Egyptian Goddesses*; *Lady of the Temple: Ancient Hymns for Nephthys*; and *Solar Flares and Sunbeams: An Anthology for Ra*. She is the editor of and a contributor to the anthology *She Who Speaks Through Silence: An Anthology for Nephthys*. Her poetry has been previously published in various anthologies. She lives with tons of books and her anti-social feline companion. You can find more of her work at her blog: http://fiercelybrightone.com

Rebecca Buchanan is the editor of the Pagan literary ezine, *Eternal Haunted Summer*, and the editor-in-chief of *Bibliotheca Alexandrina*. She is a regular contributor to the online journal, *EvOke: Witchcraft*Paganism*Lifestyle*. Her short stories and poems have been published in a wide variety of venues, a complete list of which can be found at *Eternal Haunted Summer*.

Samuel David is a Mesopotamian polytheist, artist, writer, researcher, and educator. His first book is awaiting publication with *Nephilim Press*. Once published, this book, and those which follow, will offer readers the opportunity to initiate themselves into a Mesopotamian mystery tradition akin to that of the mystery traditions of Isis, Persephone, Orpheus, and Dionysus in Greece. He is also involved with the Temple of Sumer and networks with fellow Mesopotamian polytheists and pagans across the world, keeping the spiritual traditions of the Mesopotamian people relevant in the modern world. His presentations at local pagan festivals, national, and international conventions, include lectures, rituals, and workshops. His adaptation of "The Descent of Inanna" is slated for inclusion as classroom material for California State University, Los Angeles' ancient history syllabus in 2020.

Ashley Dioses is a writer of dark fantasy, horror, and weird poetry from southern California. Her debut collection of dark traditional poetry, *Diary of a Sorceress*, was released from *Hippocampus Press* in 2017. Her second collection of early works, *The Withering*, is forthcoming from *Gehenna and Hinnom Books* this autumn. Her poetry has appeared in *Weird Fiction Review, Spectral Realms, Weirdbook Magazine*, and elsewhere. Her poem "Carathis," appeared in Ellen Datlow's full recommended *Best Horror of the Year* Volume Seven list. She has also appeared in the *Horror Writers Association Poetry Showcase* 2016 for her poem "Ghoul Mistress." She is currently an Active Member in the HWA and a member of the SFPA. Aside from writing, her other passions include martial arts and delving into esoteric and occult studies. She blogs at fiendlover.blogspot.com.

Clarabelle Fields previously wrote as Belle DiMonté, with work featured in *Swords and Sorcery Magazine, Danse Macabre, The Moon*, and *Eternal Haunted Summer*, among others. More recently, her work has appeared or is forthcoming in *Barren Magazine, Corvid Queen*, and *Enheduanna*. Her poetry collection, *Perigee Moon*, a collection of spiritual poems focusing on Nature, Diana, and the night sky, is forthcoming in November 2019. Clarabelle holds a BA in classical languages and is currently pursuing an interdisciplinary master's degree that blends creative writing and classics together. You can find out more about her and her work at www.clarabellefields.wordpress.com.

Nancy Byrne Iannucci is the author of *Temptation of Wood* (*Nixes Mate Review*). Her poems have appeared or are forthcoming in a number of publications including *Gargoyle, 8 Poems, Glass: A Journal of Poetry (Poets Resist), Typehouse Literary Magazine, Three Drops from a Cauldron, Hobo Camp Review, Allegro,* and *Clementine Unbound.* Nancy is a Long Island, New York native who now resides in Troy, New York where she teaches history and lives poetry.

Todd Jackson has self-published a volume of poems, *Ouranion.* He has presented on the God Apollon at Pantheacon, and on Greco-Buddhism at Las Vegas Pagan Pride.

Marie C Lecrivain is a poet, publisher, and ordained priestess in the Ecclesia Gnostica Catholica, the ecclesiastical arm of Ordo Templi Orientis. Her work has been published in *Nonbinary Review, Orbis, Pirene's Fountain,* and many other journals. She's the author of several books of poetry and fiction, and recent editor of *Gondal Heights: A Bronte Tribute Anthology (Sybaritic Press).*

Gerri Leen lives in Northern Virginia and originally hails from Seattle. In addition to being an avid reader, she's passionate about horse racing, tea, ASMR vids, and creating weird tacos. She has work appearing in *Nature, Galaxy's Edge, Escape Pod, Daily Science Fiction, Cast of Wonders,* and others. She's edited several anthologies for independent presses, is finishing some longer projects, and is a member of SFWA and HWA. See more at gerrileen.com.

Mark J. Mitchell was born in Chicago and grew up Catholic in southern California. He is very fond of baseball, Miles Davis, Kafka and Dante. His latest chapbook, *Music for the Other Voices,* is available from *Finishing Line Press.* A full-length collection of poems, *Starting from Tu Fu,* was just published by from *Encircle Publications* in September. His novel, *The Magic War,* is available from *Loose Leaves Publishing.* He studied at Santa Cruz under Raymond Carver and George Hitchcock. His work has appeared in several anthologies and hundreds of periodicals. He lives with his wife, activist and documentarian Joan Juster, and makes his living pointing out pretty things in San Francisco. A meager online presence can be found at https://www.facebook.com/MarkJMitchellwriter.

James B. Nicola has been a frequent contributor to Bibliotheca Alexandrina anthologies. His poetry and prose have also appeared in the *Antioch, Southwest, Green Mountains,* and *Atlanta Reviews; Rattle; Barrow Street; Tar River;* and *Poetry East,* garnering two *Willow Review* awards, a Dana Literary award, and six Pushcart nominations. His full-length collections are *Manhattan Plaza* (2014), *Stage to Page* (2016), *Wind in the Cave* (2017), *Out of Nothing: Poems of Art and Artists* (2018) and

Quickening: Poems from Before and Beyond (2019). His nonfiction book *Playing the Audience* won a *Choice* award. A Yale graduate, he is facilitator for the Hell's Kitchen International Writers' Roundtable at Manhattan's Columbus Library: walk-ins welcome.

Tahni J. Nikitins studied Comparative Literature and Creative Writing and spent a year exploring spiritual and cultural pursuits in Sweden. Her published works include "Only a Dream" in the anthology *Terror Politico*, "Is It Any Wonder" published in the 2017 edition of *A Beautiful Renaissance*, and "A Letter to Njörðr, signed Sigyn" in the devotional *Between Wind and Water*. She is currently working on revisions for her first novel.

Shirl Sazynski is a Norse mystic, and, like Frigg, a völva (Norse witch-priestess), mother, artist and storyteller. As the Gods taught her, she teaches their magic and mysteries, particularly the fate- and time-bending arts of seið trance-magic, shifting the web of wyrd and oörlog (causality) for both individuals and bloodlines, present, past and future. Their teachings are passed on in the One-Eyed Cat column and blog for *Witches and Pagans* magazine, through workshops, privately to students– and sometimes in the form of story or poem, as Gerd taught this one. Both her art and writing have appeared in numerous mundane and spiritual

venues, including: *Sacred Hoop, Sagewoman, Witches and Pagans, Idunna, Eternal Haunted Summer*, multiple literary magazines and newspapers, books from Neos Alexandrina (*The Far-Shining One: A Devotional to Spirits of the Sun* and *Les Cabinets des Polytheistes: An Anthology of Pagan Fairy Tales, Folktales, and Nursery Rhymes*) and a massive multiplayer video game.
Learn more about contacting the Norse Gods to learn from them directly and the path to becoming a volva on Facebook at /staffandcup and at staffandcup.com.

Nick Thompson writes: I have been a writer for a long time. I love writing poems to express what I am feeling. I have been in and out if prison for a very long time.

Originally from the pine-spangled coast of Maine, **Sarah Yasin** presently lives inland where she mentors writers and facilitates writing retreats. Her poetry can be found in various publications, including *J Journal* and the *Horror Writers Association Poetry Showcase*.

Lee Clark Zumpe, an entertainment editor with Tampa Bay Newspapers, earned his bachelor's in English at the University of South Florida. He began writing poetry and fiction in the early 1990s. His work has regularly appeared in a variety of literary journals and genre magazines over the last two decades. Publication credits include *Tiferet, Zillah, The Ugly Tree, Modern Drunkard Magazine, Red Owl, Jones Av., Main Street Rag, Space & Time, Mythic Delirium* and *Weird Tales*. Lee lives on the west coast of Florida with his wife and daughter.

Ptolemy Soter, the first Makedonian ruler of Egypt, established the library at Alexandria to collect all of the world's learning in a single place. His scholars compiled definitive editions of the Classics, translated important foreign texts into Greek, and made monumental strides in science, mathematics, philosophy and literature. By some accounts over a million scrolls were housed in the famed library, and though it has long since perished due to the ravages of war, fire, and human ignorance, the image of this great institution has remained as a powerful inspiration down through the centuries.

To help promote the revival of traditional polytheistic religions we have launched a series of books dedicated to the ancient gods of Greece and Egypt. The library is a collaborative effort drawing on the combined resources of the different elements within the modern Hellenic and Kemetic communities, in the hope that we can come together to praise our gods and share our diverse understandings, experiences and approaches to the divine.

A list of our current and forthcoming titles can be found on the following page. For more information on the Bibliotheca, our submission requirements for upcoming devotionals, or to learn about our organization, please visit us at neosalexandria.org.

Sincerely,

The Editorial Board
of the Library of Neos Alexandria

Current Titles

Written in Wine: A Devotional Anthology for Dionysos

Dancing God: Poetry of Myths and Magicks

Goat Foot God

Longing for Wisdom: The Message of the Maxims

The Phillupic Hymns

Unbound: A Devotional Anthology for Artemis

Waters of Life: A Devotional Anthology for Isis and Serapis

Bearing Torches: A Devotional Anthology for Hekate

Queen of the Great Below: An Anthology in Honor of Ereshkigal

From Cave to Sky: A Devotional Anthology in Honor of Zeus

Out of Arcadia: A Devotional Anthology for Pan

Anointed: A Devotional Anthology for the Deities of the Near and Middle East

The Scribing Ibis: An Anthology of Pagan Fiction in Honor of Thoth

Queen of the Sacred Way: A Devotional Anthology in Honor of Persephone

Unto Herself: A Devotional Anthology for Independent Goddesses

The Shining Cities: An Anthology of Pagan Science Fiction

Guardian of the Road: A Devotional Anthology in Honor of Hermes

Harnessing Fire: A Devotional Anthology in Honor of Hephaestus

Beyond the Pillars: An Anthology of Pagan Fantasy

Queen of Olympos: A Devotional Anthology for Hera and Iuno

A Mantle of Stars: A Devotional Anthology in Honor of the Queen of Heaven

Crossing the River: An Anthology in Honor of Sacred Journeys

Ferryman of Souls: A Devotional for Charon

By Blood, Bone, and Blade: A Tribute to the Morrigan

Potnia: An Anthology in Honor of Demeter

The Queen of the Sky Who Rules Over All the Gods: A Devotional Anthology in Honor of Bast

From the Roaring Deep: A Devotional for Poseidon and the Spirits of the Sea

Daughter of the Sun: A Devotional Anthology in Honor of Sekhmet

Seasons of Grace: A Devotional in Honor of the Muses, the Charites, and the Horae

Lunessence: A Devotional for Selene

Les Cabinets des Polythéistes: An Anthology of Pagan Fairy Tales, Folktales, and Nursery Rhymes

With Lyre and Bow: A Devotional in Honor of Apollo

Garland of the Goddess: Tales and Poems of the Feminine Divine

The Dark Ones: Tales and Poems of the Shadow Gods

First and Last: A Devotional for Hestia

Dauntless: A Devotional in Honor of Ares and Mars

Blood and Roses: A Devotional for Aphrodite and Venus

At the Gates of Dawn and Dusk: A Devotional for Aurora, Eos, and the Hesperides

The Diviner's Handbook: Writings on Ancient and Modern Divination Practices

Lord of the Carnelian Temple: A Devotional in Honor of Sobek

A Silver Sun and Inky Clouds: A Devotional for Djehuty and Set

Ascendant: Modern Essays on Polytheism and Theology

The Far-Shining One: A Devotional for the Spirits of the Sun

Circe's Cauldron: Pagan Poems and Tales of Magic and Witchcraft

Ascendant II: Theology for Modern Polytheists

Forthcoming Titles

Lord of the Horizon: A Devotional in Honor of Horus

Lady of the Sycamore: A Devotional in Honor of Hathor

Among Satyrs and Nymphs: A Devotional Anthology to Hellenic Nature Spirits

Mother of Mountains: A Devotional for Cybele and Attis

The Host of Many: Hades and His Retinue

Polytheistic Religion and Practice Volume One: Reflections and Essays

In a Shadow'd Mirror: Pagan Tales of Fantasy and Horror

BIBLIOTHECA ALEXANDRINA

www.ingramcontent.com/pod-product-compliance
Lightning Source LLC
Chambersburg PA
CBHW071315150726
47997CB00002B/489